Britain 1895–1918

Contents

Dedication

Keith Randell (1943–2002)

The *Access to History* series was conceived and developed by Keith, who created a series to 'cater for students as they are, not as we might wish them to be'. He leaves a living legacy of a series that for over 20 years has provided a trusted, stimulating and well-loved accompaniment to post-16 study. Our aim with these new editions is to continue to offer students the best possible support for their studies.

Introduction

The period 1895–1918 was one of the most turbulent periods of British political history. During that time both of the main political parties, the Liberals and the Conservatives, suffered fluctuating fortunes and underwent traumatic changes:

- In 1906 the Liberal Party won a general election victory on such a scale that its political position seemed assured for the future.
- In the same election a new political force, the Labour Party, secured a foothold in the House of Commons.
- The issue of **female suffrage** was transformed from an obscure issue into a national crusade that challenged the political system and defied the rule of law.
- The House of Lords, which had regarded itself for so long as the guardian of the constitution, was reduced to a shadow of its former power and prestige.
- Welfare legislation raised government intervention to new and unprecedented heights.
- Irish affairs plunged political life into turmoil and even seemed to threaten a civil war within the British Isles.
- Disputes between employers and trade unions, often with the government sandwiched uncomfortably between them, brought class conflicts to the surface.

Unionism

Before the 1906 general election, the political world had been dominated by an alliance between the Conservative Party and those Liberal Unionists who had split from Gladstone over the issue of Irish Home Rule in 1886. So strong did this theme of '**Unionism**' become that, for a time, the term 'Conservative Party' almost fell out of use.

Liberalism

Liberalism, too, underwent a dramatic change. The Liberal Party that won the general election in 1906 was a very different one from that which had been led by Gladstone. Many active Liberal supporters had defected to the Unionist side, including, in particular, many from the world of industry and commerce who abandoned their traditional liberalism for the apparent safety of the Conservatives or Liberal Unionists. Their defections were partly the result of increasing signs of **radicalism** within the Liberal Party, which was gradually intervening more in social issues.

This 'New Liberalism' seemed far removed from the largely non-interventionist and individualist traditions of Gladstonian Liberalism. The huge scale of the Liberal Party's victory in the 1906 general election guaranteed many new faces among the ranks of Liberal MPs. The 'New Liberal' element among them ensured that the traditional Liberal emphasis on the importance of individual liberty and self-reliance would increasingly give way to demands for social welfare.

The Future of the Nation

The political rivalry between Liberalism and Unionism took shape in a period of increasing concern about the whole question of Britain's future as a nation, a great power and an empire. The stability of the nation was threatened most seriously and immediately by the Irish Question. Unionism was based on the assumption that Irish Home Rule would prove to be merely the prelude to a complete separation of Ireland from Great Britain. Some politicians saw 'Home Rule all round' (i.e. for Wales and Scotland as well as Ireland) as the solution. The Birmingham-based radical leader Joseph Chamberlain suggested this in 1886 in response to Gladstone's adoption of the policy of Irish Home Rule.

However, others believed that such a development would threaten the whole concept of the British Empire and lead to its disintegration. If that happened, it was argued, Britain in the future would be condemned to decline to the status of a second-rate power. Such concerns about the future of the Home Countries and the Empire inevitably raised the question – just how secure was Britain's status as a 'Great Power'?

The Impact of the First World War

This question of Britain's position as a 'Great Power' was answered in the short term by the First World War, which began in August 1914. As a result of victory in war Britain's global responsibilities were increased. The threat of German domination in Europe was removed at least for the time being. British financial strength was not seriously damaged. Internationally, Britain seemed to have achieved a new peak of power and influence. Domestically, however, the war had set great changes in motion. The Liberal Party that had dominated government since 1905 was weakened. The Conservative Party had revived in strength. The Labour Party would emerge as the alternative party of government to the Conservatives.

Radicalism
Radicalism was a term applied generally to those who believed that the political, social and economic systems of the country needed reform of a very significant degree – changing very basic things such as how poverty was relieved or who should have the right to vote.

Key terms

1 Lord Salisbury and the Unionist Ascendancy 1895–1905

POINTS TO CONSIDER

Unionism was a description of the political identity of those who opposed the policy of Home Rule for Ireland as proposed by Gladstone in 1886. The term the 'Unionist Party' grew out of the close association between the Conservatives, led by Lord Salisbury, and the 'Liberal Unionists', led by Joseph Chamberlain, who split away from the main Liberal Party in protest against Gladstone's insistence on Home Rule. The period 1895–1905 was an important time of transition for the two main parties and also saw the emergence of the Labour Party. This chapter considers the period through the following themes:

- The career of Lord Salisbury and his importance as a Conservative leader
- Britain's status as a world power: its economy and the issue of social reform
- New Imperialism
- The Boer War
- The reasons for the decline and catastrophic defeat of the Unionist Party in 1906.

Key dates

1895	Salisbury, leader of the Conservative Party, forms a coalition 'Unionist' government with the Liberal Unionists, led by Joseph Chamberlain
1896	Jameson's Raid, attempting to overthrow the government of Transvaal, causes an international scandal
1897	Workmen's Compensation Act gives limited help to some categories of workers injured in their workplaces
1899	Boer War begins
1900	General election results in overwhelming victory for the Unionist Government

1901 Queen Victoria dies
1902 British victory in the Boer War
Lord Salisbury resigns as Prime Minister and is
replaced by his nephew, A.J. Balfour
The Education Act
1903 Joseph Chamberlain announces his policy of
'Tariff Reform and Imperial Preference' and
resigns from the Cabinet to lead a national
campaign
1905 Balfour resigns and the king appoints the Liberal
leader, Sir Henry Campbell-Bannerman, as Prime
Minister
1906 The Liberal Party wins a massive victory in the
general election

1 | Lord Salisbury

Key question
How did Lord
Salisbury come to
dominate British
politics?

Lord Robert Cecil (Salisbury) was born in 1830. He was the
second son of the then Lord Salisbury and therefore not
originally destined to succeed to his father's title. He had the
usual educational experience of one of his class – public school
(Eton), and then on to Oxford, but there things began to go
wrong. Before he could complete his degree he suffered a
breakdown and was sent abroad by his family to recover his
health. On his return he married against his father's wishes and,
as a result, found himself forced to live on only a minimal
allowance by his standards. Needing to make his own way in the
world, he used his social position to enter politics, becoming an
MP at the age of 23.

MPs at that time had no salary, so Salisbury was obliged to find
some method of earning a living to supplement his allowance. He
hit upon the idea of writing political articles and proved to be
very successful at it. He soon became a respected authority on
constitutional matters and, in particular, on foreign policy. He
wrote regularly for the most famous conservative magazine of the
day, *The Quarterly Review*, and was soon seen as a rising young star
of the Conservative Party.

The death of his elder brother made him the heir to the family
estates. Now using the family's second title, Viscount Cranborne,
he accepted a **Cabinet** place in Lord Derby's Conservative
Government of 1866–8 as Indian Secretary. However, when Derby
retired and was replaced by Benjamin Disraeli in 1868, he refused
to continue in office, having many times in the past criticised
Disraeli in his political articles. Also in 1868 his father died,
leaving him the title, the great family estates and a formidable
social position to add to his already strong political credibility. At
this stage he was marked out as a near certainty to lead the
Conservative Party at some point in the future.

By 1874 he had made up his differences with Disraeli and
agreed to join the new government that was formed in that year.

Lord Salisbury
dominated the
Conservative Party
and with it British
politics following the
death of Benjamin
Disraeli in 1881.

Cabinet
The highest level of
government, the
members of which
run the most
important
government
departments.

Key term

Initially he was Indian Secretary again, but in 1878 he was promoted to **Foreign Secretary** and in that same year accompanied Disraeli to one of the great diplomatic events of the nineteenth century, the Congress of Berlin. In this conference, called to avoid war between the Great Powers over Russian aggression against Turkey, Salisbury took the lead in organising the minute details of the settlement with his counterparts from Germany, France, Austria and Russia.

In 1881, when Disraeli died, Salisbury was the obvious successor. When Gladstone's government fell in 1885 he took over as Prime Minister for the first of three administrations; 1885–6, 1886–92 and 1895–1902. For most of his years as Prime Minister he combined the office with that of Foreign Secretary. He retired as Prime Minister in 1902 and died the following year. He was the last peer to hold the office of Prime Minister.

Political ideas
Conservatism

Lord Salisbury faced the central problem that all conservatives have contended with before his time and since. That is – what is it that should be 'conserved' and how best can conservation be achieved?

Like all conservatives he faced the paradox that sometimes the only way to conserve one thing is to reform or give up something else. Salisbury was a formidable politician. He realised that **Conservatism** needed a coherent and convincing response to the issues of the day. He understood that it had to appeal to the working-class voters as well as the middle and upper classes. He also saw that the working class in Britain was mainly conservative in instinct and that properly managed the system could remain stable despite its obvious social inequalities.

Fatalism

Salisbury was an intensely devout **Anglican** and this gave him a sense of inner strength and certainty that helped him to frame his ideas. He was also a fatalist. That is to say he truly believed that many things in human affairs were beyond the capacity of men to affect and that fate or destiny was a determining factor in how events turned out. It followed then that he did not have unlimited faith in the ability of governments to deal with every turn of events. He once likened conducting foreign policy, his main interest, to travelling downstream in a canoe using the paddle to fend off collisions. In other words, he did not really believe that governments or anyone else were fully in control of their destinies, only God had full control.

Salisbury had a genuine fear of what he called 'disintegration'. By this he meant the breaking up of all the things that held society and the nation together. He championed the class system as the only way to conduct a civilised society. However, he recognised the destructive potential of class conflicts and was prepared to accept some social reforms as necessary for social harmony.

Key question
What beliefs were central to Salisbury's view of government?

Key terms

Foreign Secretary
The Cabinet minister responsible for handling the country's relations with foreign powers and its responses to international events.

Conservatism
The political principle that the presentation of traditions and existing institutions should be assumed to be the objective of politics.

Anglican
One who accepts the doctrine of the Anglican Church of England.

Unionism

In the late 1880s and early 1890s he was most preoccupied by the issue of Irish **Home Rule**, which he saw as likely to bring about the disintegration of the United Kingdom and with it the Empire. To avoid this he was prepared to forge an alliance with the Liberal Unionists who had left the Liberal Party in opposition to Gladstone's policy of Irish Home Rule.

In 1895 he opted to form a coalition government with the Liberal Unionists in order to consolidate the opposition to Home Rule. General elections in 1895 and 1900 both gave the Conservative Party an overall majority which would have allowed Salisbury to avoid coalitions, but he deliberately chose not to do this because he believed that, in the long term, it was wiser to build the strongest possible barrier to Home Rule.

Home Rule
The principle that Ireland should control its own *internal* affairs within the United Kingdom.

Key term

Salisbury forms a coalition 'Unionist' government with the Liberal Unionists, led by Joseph Chamberlain: 1895

General election results in overwhelming victory for the Unionist Government: 1900

Key dates

Conclusion

His specific ideas on politics can be summarised as follows:

- The integrity of the monarchy, the Church of England and the parliamentary system of government (often referred to as the 'Institutions of State') must be preserved at all cost.
- The Empire must be preserved as the only sure guarantee that Great Britain would maintain its position as a first class power.
- Reforms should be introduced as and when they were necessary to ensure that the Institutions of State and the Empire were protected.

Although determined to work for the principles of government and society he believed in, Salisbury was not ambitious personally. He regarded governmental office as a duty to which men of his class and ability were called. Salisbury did not regard being Prime Minister as an achievement but as an unwelcome burden he was required to shoulder. In so far as he desired public office at all, he would have preferred to concentrate on being Foreign Secretary. In 1895 he even tried to persuade one of the leading Liberal Unionists, the Duke of Devonshire, to accept the post of Prime Minister, before being forced to agree that this would not be acceptable to the Conservative Party, who expected him to lead the government. When Salisbury eventually retired in 1902 it was without regret, rather with relief.

2 | A Great Power in Decline?

Concerns about Britain's future as a Great Power gathered momentum in the 1890s. They were based on four considerations.

- First, there was the question of Britain's diplomatic 'isolation' and the increasing hostility with which she was regarded by other nations. (This question is discussed in Chapter 7.)
- Second, there was the question of Britain's economic performance and the extent to which other nations were catching up with, or even overtaking, Britain as the leading manufacturing and commercial power.

Key question
How serious were the problems facing Britain at the end of the 1890s?

- Third, there was the question of the condition of the working classes in Britain and the extent to which this was undermining Britain both economically and socially.
- Finally, there was the issue of Ireland and the integrity of the United Kingdom as a unified state. (This is dealt with more fully in Chapter 6.)

Economic performance

Key question
Why were there concerns about the British economy in this period?

Concern about the performance of the British economy stemmed from the 1870s. For nearly three decades before this the economy had been growing relatively consistently, but it was suddenly beset by a series of slumps interspersed with temporary revivals. The last of these slumps ended in 1896 and was followed by a steady, if slow, period of economic expansion up to 1914, with only one downturn in the period 1907–10.

However, despite this 'recovery', the cycle of slumps over a 25-year period up to 1896 had been enough to undermine the confidence in British economic strength which had been taken for granted in the middle years of the century – a period which has been characterised as the '**Great Victorian Boom**'.

Key term

Great Victorian Boom
An expression customarily used to describe the expansion of production in agriculture and industry during the period 1850–70

Economic historians disagree about the significance of the period after 1870. At one time it was customary to refer to the last quarter of the nineteenth century as the 'Great Depression'. More recently however, most economic historians have rejected this view, preferring to describe the period as one involving a 'retardation of growth'; that is to say, a slowing down of the earlier, rapid expansion of the economy, until a lower, more sustainable pattern of growth was reached in the 1890s.

Industry
In retrospect it is easy to see that fears about the strength of the British economy in this period were exaggerated. In fact, the economy was performing in a rather erratic way. For example, the period after 1870 was precisely when Britain was emerging as the world's leading shipbuilding nation – a status she was to maintain through many trials and tribulations until the Second World War.

Output of iron and steel continued to increase, despite competition from Germany and the USA, and even the inefficient British coal industry continued to remain profitable in the years up to 1914, buoyed up by consistently increasing world demand for coal.

However, it is also true that Britain did not expand as rapidly as Germany or the USA in the newer industrial sectors, such as electrical engineering and chemical production.

Agriculture
The agricultural sector, however, faced a more difficult problem, in that cheap imports of cereals from the 1870s put pressure on British farmers and forced them to reduce their production. Even livestock farmers faced some competition as steamships with refrigerated cargo holds allowed cheap meat to be imported from abroad.

The case for a 'Great Depression' in the agricultural sector is thus more convincing than that for industry, but even so the picture was not one of unrelieved gloom. Cheaper imports of cereals meant cheaper foodstuffs for livestock farmers and in some parts of the country, farm rents actually rose in this period as profits soared. Moreover, the availability of cheaper food meant that, across the nation as a whole, the value of wages was consistently rising in real terms, despite the effects of the periodic slumps.

International trade

The most obvious, and most discussed aspect of economic performance, was the question of international trade. More specifically, there was the question of German imports and the size of the **trade gap** that began to increase after 1870. Such gaps had, however, existed even in the 1850s and were always more than covered by the value of so-called **invisible earnings** from insurance, shipping charges and banking services that brought increasingly vast profits into the British economy. London remained the commercial centre of the world and its dominance was unchallenged.

Nevertheless, having noted that much of the concern about British economic performance was exaggerated, it is important to realise that what people at the time believed to be the case is often more important to understanding that period, than what subsequent historical research and deliberation reveal to have been the case.

Unionism and social reform

What helped create concern about the condition of the working classes was the publication of evidence in 'scientific' investigations into poverty that began to appear in the 1880s. Charles Booth, a shipping magnate, published details of his investigation into the London district of Tower Hamlets in 1887. He claimed that one-third of the population was living below the **poverty line**. Booth went on to conduct a series of investigations between 1891 and 1903. His work was paralleled by the study of poverty in York undertaken by Seebohm Rowntree and published in 1901. These investigations and others, similar if less well known, were prompted partly by genuine **humanitarian** concerns and partly by violent demonstrations by unemployed men in the mid-1880s coinciding with one of the periodic economic slumps.

These investigations were also intended to provide factual evidence about poverty, in contrast to the rather emotional and sensational accounts that were becoming common in the 1880s. Their chief value was to demonstrate that unemployment and poverty could not be viewed solely as the result of vice or laziness. Indeed, one result of Booth's findings was to show clearly that the chief factor in poverty was family size and that the number of children in a family was a more significant element in determining living standards than unemployment.

Key terms

Trade gap
Where the value of items imported into the country exceed the value of exports.

Invisible earnings
Earnings from insurance premiums, shipping and brokerage fees, where no actual sale of goods was involved.

Key question
Why did social reform become an issue in this period?

Key terms

Poverty line
The level of income needed to support the minimum requirements of life in terms of food, accommodation, etc. Obviously this would vary according to family size.

Humanitarian
Concern for the human condition and especially for those thought to be unable to protect themselves.

Conditions such as in this slum in London in the 1870s led people to become concerned about poverty.

The poor physical condition of many of the would-be recruits for the Boer War of 1899–1902 added fuel to the fires of publicity that scientific investigation had stoked. It added to the idea that poverty and degradation were turning the British lower classes into some kind of subspecies. Booth had written that the:

> lives of the poor lay hidden from view behind curtains on which were painted terrible pictures; starving children, suffering women, overworked men …

His (unrelated) namesake, William Booth, the founder of the Salvation Army, published a pamphlet in 1890 entitled *In Darkest England and the Way Out*, in which he portrayed the working-class districts as more remote than darkest Africa in terms of their remoteness from the experience of the upper and middle classes. This idea that the condition of the working classes posed some kind of nameless threat to civilised standards was to prove a potent force in promoting the acceptability of **interventionist social reform**.

Responses to the problem of poverty

It was perhaps inevitable that people concerned with both the apparent economic decline of Britain and the supposed physical deterioration of the working classes should seek to establish some link between the two. The more extreme responses to the problem pressed for:

- sterilisation and **selective breeding programmes**
- bans on foreign immigration, as it was allegedly polluting the 'bloodstock' of the British race, contributing to unemployment and spreading diseases. In 1905 an "Aliens Act" was introduced aimed at refusing entry to Britain to those immigrants thought to be incapable of supporting themselves, or carrying diseases.

The idea that national efficiency was being undermined and that something needed to be done about it was embraced by a wide range of writers, from **socialists** such as Sidney and Beatrice Webb, who became leading figures in the Labour Party, to **imperialists** such as Lord Rosebery. Social reform was an obvious objective for those who argued that poverty was the main cause of the social degradation that was threatening national efficiency and the future of the British Empire.

The Education Act 1902

One particularly relevant social issue was that of popular education and the effectiveness of the system that had been put into place during Gladstone's first administration in 1870.

The idea that British education was inferior in many respects to that of other countries had long been taking shape. Most attention was usually focused on the deficiencies of British technical and scientific education compared to that offered to the general population in Germany or France. The belief that national efficiency could be promoted, or, to put it another way, that national decline could be halted by a reform of the education system was one of the reasons for the passing of a controversial Education Act by the Unionist Government in 1902.

The Duke of Devonshire, who was the Cabinet minister responsible for education, and Arthur Balfour, Salisbury's nephew and the Leader of the House of Commons, both favoured a fundamental reform of the education system. Both were impressed by the argument that an efficient and properly funded education system was essential for a modern state aiming to maintain its place in the world.

In 1902, these two men took charge of the drafting of an education bill designed to bring about a substantial measure of

Key terms

Interventionist social reform
Reforms relying on direct action by Government to enforce conditions.

Selective breeding programmes
The principle of ensuring that only those who are free from disease and hereditary defects are allowed to reproduce.

Socialist
The political principle that requires the abolition of private property in favour of public ownership.

Imperialist
The principle of territorial expansion by a country in order to strengthen its position.

Key question
What did the Education Act seek to achieve?

Key term

Nonconformist
Member of any Protestant Christian Church (i.e. not a Roman Catholic) that did not 'conform' to the teachings of the Anglican Church of England. Presbyterians, Methodists and Baptists are examples.

Key terms

Elementary education
Compulsory basic education provided up to the age of 11 or 12 for all children.

Secondary education
Further non-compulsory education, usually only undertaken by middle-class or better-off working-class children, which ended at any age up to 18.

Royal Commission
Set up to investigate a particular issue and usually to suggest a course of action. Generally composed of a mixture of politicians, interested parties and experts in whatever field under enquiry.

Key question
Why did education become a political battleground?

Key term

Anglican schools
Originally called 'National Schools', these schools provided elementary education and were sponsored by the Church of England.

reform. Lord Salisbury was dubious about it, but since he intended to retire from the premiership in the near future he did not oppose the idea. Joseph Chamberlain was also unenthusiastic, not because he undervalued education, but because, as a **Nonconformist** he could anticipate the storm that would result from any attempt at government interference in the role played by the Churches in the provision of education, or from any attempt to fund Anglican schools from local rates. However, Chamberlain could not overrule Balfour who was the clear successor to Salisbury as Prime Minister.

The purpose of the Education Act
The purpose of the 1902 Education Act was to provide a new structure for both **elementary** and **secondary education** under local authority control. The school boards that had been set up under the 1870 Act had legal powers only in respect of elementary provision. Over the years, many Boards had gone well beyond their authority by providing secondary education as well. This meant that they were using ratepayers' money without any legal basis.

The situation came to a head in 1901, when a court case was brought against the London School Board for the recovery of expenses they had spent in providing secondary education courses. The judge ruled against the Board on the grounds that the 1870 Act implied that rates could be spent only on children taking basic subjects. This judgement led to severe restrictions on school board spending on technical, evening and adult classes, all of which had been expanding in recent years and all of which could be argued to be contributing to the creation of a better educated population.

At central level, responsibility for both elementary and secondary education had been assumed by a Board of Education, created in 1899 on the advice of a **Royal Commission**. Balfour and Devonshire therefore proposed to extend this principle to the local level.

Opposition to the Act
The Education Act of 1902 was passed amidst great controversy, as Salisbury and Chamberlain had foreseen.

The Act swept away the old school boards and created Local Education Authorities under the County and Borough Councils. These LEAs had responsibility for both elementary and secondary education and were also required to support the voluntary (Church) schools out of the rates. This latter provision caused the political controversy. Nonconformists were outraged by the idea of ratepayers' money being used to support the **Anglican schools**. The Liberals, conscious of their traditional political support among the Nonconformists, fought the proposal every inch of the way in the House of Commons and a great national campaign of opposition began, in which the Welsh radical, David Lloyd George, himself a Nonconformist, took a leading role.

Profile: Joseph Chamberlain 1836–1914

1836	– Born in London
1873–5	– Mayor of Birmingham
1876	– Became a Liberal MP
1880	– Became a member of Cabinet as President of the Board of Trade
1886	– Resigned from government over issue of Home Rule
1889	– Became leader of the Liberal Unionists
1895	– Joined the coalition government of Lord Salisbury as Colonial Secretary
1903	– Announced his policy of 'Tariff Reform and Imperial Preference' and resigned from the Cabinet to lead a national campaign
1906	– Withdrew from public life
1914	– Died

Early life

Joseph Chamberlain was born in London in 1836 into a comfortable, but not exceptionally wealthy, middle-class family. They were Nonconformists belonging to the Unitarian Church denomination and Chamberlain's education was in small private schools that were acceptable to the religious viewpoint of his family. He did not therefore have access to the traditional training ground for high-profile politicians – major public school followed by Oxford or Cambridge.

At 16 he left school and entered the family business and at 18 he left for Birmingham to work in a new business venture in which his father had made an investment of several hundred pounds.

Entry into politics

Chamberlain eventually took charge of the business and turned it into a corporate empire. By the time he was in his thirties he was a millionaire and looking to leave his business affairs to managers while he concentrated on politics. He was the first major national politician to make his name in local politics and then transfer to the greater stage.

In 1873–5 he was mayor of Birmingham, a city which he transformed with a series of major public works such as slum clearance and bringing in gas and water supplies, street lighting and civic buildings. His work there made his a national figure and he became one of the city's MPs in 1876.

Cabinet minister

His reputation as a radical champion of reforms to benefit the working classes put him at the forefront of the radical liberals and, in 1880, Gladstone had little option but to offer him a post in the Cabinet as President of the Board of Trade.

Seeing himself as a (not too distant) future leader of the Liberal Party, Chamberlain was impatient with Gladstone's reluctance to promote him to a more senior post, but, despite snubs from Gladstone, who did not consider Chamberlain a 'gentleman', he refused to resign from the government until 1886 when Gladstone declared his intention to bring in Home Rule for Ireland. Chamberlain saw this as potentially leading to the break up of the United Kingdom and the Empire, which he already saw as being of central importance in his ideas. He also thought that Home Rule was a distraction from the more important issues of social reform.

The Liberal Unionists

From 1889 Chamberlain became the leader of the group of Liberal Unionists that had split with Gladstone. He gradually drew closer to the Conservatives, believing that the party that had brought in many social reforms under Disraeli in the 1870s could be the vehicle for his own ambitions.

In 1895 he joined the coalition government of Lord Salisbury as Colonial Secretary. His imperial policies aimed at promoting unity within the empire made him a controversial figure and, in 1903, he left the government to campaign for the end of free trade and the setting up of a system of general tariffs with preferential treatment for the Empire. In 1906 he suffered a stroke that eventually led to his complete physical incapacity and withdrawal from public life. He died in 1914.

Attempts at compromise failed completely. Joseph Chamberlain suggested avoiding using the rates altogether by increasing government grants, but the cost of the Boer War ruled out that idea. Another possibility was a clause introducing an 'adoptive principle', under which it would have been left to local authorities to decide whether or not to use the rates in this way. Balfour was against this on the grounds that it meant that this issue would always be a political one and lead to endless arguments at local level as well as leaving some Anglican schools at the mercy of hostile local councils. A good many Tories sympathised with Balfour's position and the clause was removed.

Political effects of the Education Act

The passing of the 1902 Education Act cost the Unionist government dearly in political terms. There were over 70,000 prosecutions for non-payment of rates in the following year and in Wales, where Nonconformity was strong, the opposition was bitter. The Liberals reaped the benefit of a great revival in Nonconformity, which had been markedly on the decline. The issue also enabled the Liberals to mend the party split that had occurred over the Boer War (see page 19).

Within the government itself the Education Act had a divisive effect. One of the fundamental realities of the Unionist Coalition was its bringing together of Anglican and Nonconformist opinion – the latter being most obviously represented by the prominent position of Chamberlain. The maintenance of a kind of status quo had been central to this understanding. Chamberlain was deeply embarrassed with his own Nonconformist supporters by the controversy and it undermined his own feelings of obligation towards his Conservative partners, not to rock the political boat with his own developing ideas.

Despite Chamberlain's radical views, the Unionist Government failed to get to grips with the social problems that were being identified during this period. The 1902 Education Act was the only piece of legislation in the period 1895–1905 that made a fundamental change in a major area of social policy.

Other reforms

The only other notable reform was introduced in 1897 in the form of a Workmen's Compensation Act that enabled workers injured at work to claim compensation from their employers. Even this was limited in that it did not apply to some important categories of workers such as agricultural labourers, seamen and domestic servants.

Chamberlain was committed to a much wider range of reforms to benefit the working classes and Salisbury was prepared to back him provided the reforms were not so radical as to be a serious threat to his party's unity. In particular, Chamberlain was keen to introduce a system of old age pensions, but despite much discussion nothing materialised. Chamberlain's failure can be explained as follows:

- He was increasingly convinced that social reforms on the scale he envisaged could only be funded through imperial development. He therefore believed that his main task was to focus on the Empire and to strengthen it politically and economically. It was for this reason that he had chosen to be Colonial Secretary in preference to the posts of Home Secretary or Chancellor of the Exchequer that Salisbury had offered him. Either of these offices would have made it much easier for Chamberlain to oversee social reform policies.
- Because Chamberlain was not in a government post that allowed him to focus directly on social reforms, the issues tended to be sidelined into committees in which those less enthusiastic about reform were able to delay things. For example, the question of old age pensions was referred to a commission of enquiry that made no progress other than to consider the probable expense.
- In 1899 the Boer War began and the mounting cost of this conflict meant that the costs of social reforms became the overriding issue.
- By the time the Boer War ended, Chamberlain had become totally convinced that social reform was dependent on the creation of wealth through the development of the Empire. This, he had come to believe, required an end to the policy of **free trade** which had been adopted in the middle years of the century and the reintroduction of **protective tariffs**. He left the government in 1903 to campaign for this programme and without him the Unionists lost all focus on social reform (see page 23).

← Key question
What other reforms were pushed for in this period?

Key dates

Workmen's Compensation Act: 1897

Boer War begins: 1899

Key terms

Free trade
An economic policy in which taxes are not applied (or only minimally applied) to imports and exports and no barriers are imposed on the import or export of goods.

Protective tariffs
Taxes on imports to make them more expensive and thus 'protect' domestic produce.

Summary diagram: A Great Power in decline?	
Symptoms	**Cures?**
• Economic depression • Performance of other countries • Trade gap • Condition of the working classes • Poor-quality education	• Stick with free trade or use economic protection? • Rely on self-improvement or bring in social reforms? • Education Act 1902

Key question
What was New
Imperialism?

3 | New Imperialism

New Imperialism can be defined as the idea that the British Empire should be seen as an economic asset that needed to be properly managed and developed both politically and economically. It contrasted with the more conventional views of the role of the Empire:

- That it was a costly inconvenience – but needed for national prestige and Britain's image as a Great Power.
- That it provided a useful outlet for surplus population and investment.
- That it was a moral obligation carrying with it the duty to spread enlightened Christian civilisation to other peoples.

In contrast to these views there was an altogether more positive, enthusiastic and nationalistic approach that drew together various aspects of the more conventional ideas. The development of this New Imperialism can be traced back to the 1860s and the ideas of enthusiasts for empire such as the historian J.A. Froude and the radical liberal politician Sir Charles Dilke.

In 1868 Dilke published a book entitled *Greater Britain* in which he advocated the expansion and development of empire and emphasised the cultural ties that united the 'English-speaking peoples'. This was highly influential and sparked off a revival of interest in the Empire and the idea of imperial expansion.

The 1870s saw the start of a new phase of rapid expansion by the other European imperial powers, most notably the French. This saw a 'Scramble for Africa' in which large areas of the continent fell under European control. It was impossible for Britain to stand aloof from this and soon Britain's imperial possessions were outstripping all the other powers.

In 1876 the importance of India within the British Empire was marked by the creation of the title Empress of India to add to the titles of Queen Victoria. Though some cynics remarked that it was a title better suited to a railway locomotive, it was a sign that the Empire was being taken more seriously.

In the 1880s New Imperialism was given a further impetus by the work of J.R. Seeley, a Professor of Modern History at Cambridge University. Seeley delivered a series of lectures in 1881 entitled *The Expansion of England*. These were published as a book in 1883. In this Seeley offered the classic statement that defined New Imperialism in the form of a question that proposed an awesome challenge for the future:

> Will the English race, which is divided by so many oceans, making full use of modern scientific inventions, devise some form of organisation like that of the United States, under which full liberty and solid union may be reconciled with unbounded territorial expansion?

This goal became the essential objective in the 1890s for those who increasingly came to believe that only through an integrated and developed empire could Britain maintain itself as a world power in the coming twentieth century. The greatest political figure to embrace the vision of New Imperialism was Joseph Chamberlain.

4 | The Boer War 1899–1902

The vision for Africa

Key question
Why did war break out in southern Africa in 1899?

Chamberlain became Colonial Secretary in 1895 with a mission to unify the Empire politically and integrate and develop it economically. Nowhere was there a greater challenge to his vision than in southern Africa. Britain had ruled the Cape Colony since taking it from Holland during the Napoleonic Wars. Under British control it had expanded in size and wealth and become a self-governing colony.

The Prime Minister of the Cape, Cecil Rhodes, like Chamberlain a self-made millionaire, had a vision of which Chamberlain approved. This was the expansion of British influence throughout Africa, linking the continent in an unbroken chain of territory from south to north. Standing in the way of this dream, however, were the states of Transvaal and Orange Free State that were settled by **Boers**. The Orange Free State was small and agriculturally based and in no way a threat to British domination of southern Africa. Transvaal, however, was a different proposition. The discovery of gold in the 1880s made it wealthy and attracted to it miners and engineers from all over the world.

The Boer government of Transvaal welcomed its newly found wealth but feared the political impact of the influx of foreign workers and businessmen, many of whom were British. It passed laws to restrict the political rights of these workers and imposed heavier taxation on them. At the same time it set about arming itself and secretly forging links with the rising imperial power of Germany, which it saw as a possible protector against the British.

Boers
Descendants of the original Dutch-speaking farmers who had first colonised the Cape and who had migrated north to escape the rule of the British. Boer in Dutch means farmer.

Key term

The first Boer War

There was already a history of hostility. In 1877, faced with the possibility of attack by an aggressive Zulu army, the Boers had agreed to be annexed into the British Empire. Once Britain had eliminated the Zulu threat by 1879, however, they reneged on their decision and reclaimed their independence. There was a brief conflict in 1881–2, sometimes known as the first Boer War, after which Britain agreed to allow Transvaal to leave the Empire. This independence, however, was subject to the proviso that it should not engage in any relationships with foreign powers unless Britain had prior consultation and gave approval. The Boers agreed to this in 1884 in a settlement known as the London Convention.

The Jameson Raid

Rhodes was secretly determined that the Transvaal must be brought back under British control once and for all. In 1896 he hatched a plot to bring down the Transvaal government using the resources of the British South Africa Company, which he controlled and which had an armed police force at its disposal. Rhodes's brother Frank was to lead a revolt in Transvaal itself, while a senior figure in the Company, Dr Leander Jameson, led a force of men into Transvaal to 'restore order'.

The attempted *coup*, which became known as the 'Jameson Raid', was a fiasco:

- Jameson and Frank Rhodes were arrested.
- Cecil Rhodes was exposed as the instigator and had to resign as Prime Minister of the Cape Colony.
- Chamberlain himself was accused of complicity in the plot and had to endure a parliamentary inquiry that ultimately concluded that there was no evidence of his involvement.
- Worse still, the incident provoked a confrontation with Germany when Kaiser Wilhelm II sent a telegram to the Transvaal government congratulating it on defeating the *coup* without having to ask for help from Germany. The implication that Germany saw itself as free to intervene in such a matter forced the British Government to deploy the North Sea Fleet and ask for 'clarification' of the German position, which in diplomatic parlance, meant asking for an apology. The Germans did apologise but the incident soured relations and made Chamberlain and those who shared his New Imperialist vision even more determined to bring Transvaal to heel.

Declaration of war

Between 1896 and 1899 discussions continued between the British Government and the Boer Government of Transvaal over the position of British workers who were denied full political rights in Transvaal. Chamberlain did not help the cause of compromise by appointing Lord Milner, a hard-line imperialist, to the key post of High Commissioner of the Cape, effectively the British Government's representative. Milner was not interested in a settlement unless it was one dictated on British terms.

By late 1899 relations had deteriorated to the point where both sides expected a conflict at any moment. It was the Boers who lost their nerve first. In October 1899 President Paul Kruger of the Transvaal declared war on Britain and launched immediate strikes into British territory in the hope of securing a quick victory. It was precisely the miscalculation Chamberlain, Milner and the advocates of New Imperialism had been waiting for.

Initial setbacks

Initially the war went badly for Britain. Despite the fact that the Boers had struck first, most world opinion outside the Empire was united in seeing Britain as the true aggressor against a small nation. Even within Britain there was a vocal minority in the Liberal Party that opposed the war and became known as 'pro-Boers' for their trouble.

Not only that, but the military conflict itself was a disaster for Britain in the first months of the war as inadequacies in military organisation, combined with Boer determination and ruthlessness, produced a series of defeats. The Boer forces surrounded the towns of Ladysmith and Mafeking and laid sieges. However, these were eventually raised by the British Army as their superior resources in terms of manpower and weapons started to have an effect. By the end of 1900 it was clear that the initial British military difficulties were over and that the Boers would be defeated.

Key question
What problems arose for Britain during the course of the war?

British victory

Eventual and inevitable British victory came in 1902. However, the manner of the victory left a sour taste. Facing defeat in the form of overwhelming numbers and resources the Boers resorted to hit-and-run guerrilla tactics to resist. To combat this the British resorted to rounding up Boer civilian non-combatants and 'concentrating' them in large camps. The motives for this were not entirely without credit. The principal consideration was to deprive the guerrilla fighters of bases in their home to which they could return to rest and regroup.

British victory in the Boer War: 1902

Key date

The siege of Ladysmith 1899.

Key term

'Scorched earth' policy
A military tactic in which buildings, crops, livestock, factories, etc. are destroyed in order to deprive the opposition of resources.

Removing the civilians made it possible to adopt a **'scorched earth' policy** to counter guerrilla warfare. This was the only policy that could be made effective as a counter to the Boer tactics. Also it was assumed that bringing the Boer women, children and elderly men into a protected environment would reduce the risk of civilian casualties. The policy, however, went disastrously wrong. There was a total failure on the part of the military authorities to understand the requirements of such camps in terms of food, sanitation and medical provision. The result was that diseases such as typhus and cholera spread like wildfire in the camps, bringing thousands of deaths. The British press ran a critical campaign exposing the camps, and the fate of Boer civilians in them became a national and international scandal.

When the war ended in 1902 there was relatively little sense of national euphoria, rather a sense of relief. The war had been costly, embarrassing and divisive. There was strong feeling that the peace settlement needed to be one on which a better basis of Anglo-Boer relations could be built in the future. The Peace of Vereeniging of 1902 reflected this desire. Under its terms Transvaal and Orange Free State were absorbed into the British Empire but with promise of self-government (made good in 1907) and with generous provisions for reparations from Britain to help repair the damage done by the war.

Key question
What were the political effects of the Boer War?

Impact of the war

For New Imperialism the experience of the Boer War was mixed. On the one hand the military problems of the early stages of the war had raised doubts about Britain's status as a military power. The political divisions at home and the moral scandal of the camps had combined to put imperialism in a poor light. However, on the positive side, the Empire had pulled together to meet and resolve the crisis. The victorious war effort had been based on the use of volunteers from Britain and other parts of the Empire. The peace was generous and had the effect of reconciling at least some Boers to the prospect of permanent membership of the Empire.

In 1910, Transvaal and Orange Free State were sufficiently pro-British to agree to become members of a new Union of South Africa, which brought them together with the British-dominated areas of the Cape and Natal. In 1914, South Africa joined in the war against Germany. One former Boer General, Jan Smuts, even joined the Imperial War Cabinet in London in 1917.

Even so, on the central New Imperialist issues of closer economic and political integration, no real progress was made. Chamberlain's campaign for tariff reform (see pages 21–3) split the Unionists and helped reunite the Liberals after their divided response to the Boer War. In the 1906 general election it was the Liberals and Labour, with their continued support for cheaper food through free trade, who convinced the voters rather than the Unionist case that the future lay with developing the Empire through economic protection.

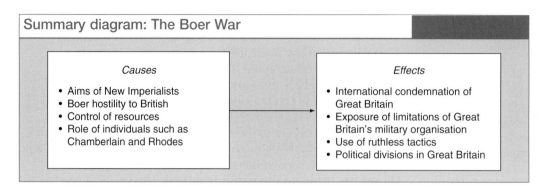

Summary diagram: The Boer War

Causes
- Aims of New Imperialists
- Boer hostility to British
- Control of resources
- Role of individuals such as Chamberlain and Rhodes

Effects
- International condemnation of Great Britain
- Exposure of limitations of Great Britain's military organisation
- Use of ruthless tactics
- Political divisions in Great Britain

5 | The Decline of the Unionists

In September 1902 Lord Salisbury retired from the premiership and was succeeded by Arthur Balfour. The death of Queen Victoria in January 1901 had released him from continuing in an office that he had come to regard as an intolerable burden. A sense of duty compelled him to remain at his post while the Boer War continued and until the new king had been crowned, but once the coronation had been held he gratefully relinquished office.

There was no question of a struggle for the succession. The only conceivable alternative to Balfour was Chamberlain and the latter knew perfectly well that he was not acceptable, as leader, to most of the Conservatives. Chamberlain accepted this situation realistically and never made any attempt to intervene, despite some press efforts to stir up a campaign on his behalf. His acceptance of Balfour, however, did not mean that he was satisfied with the state of affairs within the Unionist Government.

Chamberlain's dissatisfaction

Chamberlain's dissatisfaction stemmed from a variety of frustrations in his political life:

- He wanted to be Prime Minister but he knew that there was almost no prospect of this happening.
- Increasingly he felt that the government's lack of achievements in social policy was undermining his credibility and playing into the hands of the socialists.
- He was worried at the lack of progress, as he saw it, in ending British isolation in foreign policy (see page 131).
- Most of all, he was frustrated at the lack of progress that his plans for the unification of the Empire were making.

Since 1897 Chamberlain had made repeated efforts to advance the idea of an **imperial federation** based initially on economic union between the different countries of the Empire. So far, however, all his efforts to interest the Prime Ministers of the various countries of the Empire had failed. To Chamberlain this spelled disaster for both the Empire and the United Kingdom. He firmly believed that the future lay with large countries,

Key question
What caused the Unionists to decline in influence as a political force?

Queen Victoria dies: 1901

Key date

Imperial federation
The principle of joining several self-governing territories within the Empire into a union of equals.

Key term

possessed of large populations with access to vast natural resources. For Britain to compete with the likes of the USA and Germany there was, according to Chamberlain's analysis, no alternative but the unification of the Empire or a decline to minor international status.

By 1902 Chamberlain was little short of desperate for a political initiative. The 'triumph' of the Boer War – 'Joe's War' as it was often called – had turned sour; the Education Bill was an acute embarrassment; Chamberlain became determined to embark upon a major scheme that would seize the public's imagination, rescue Unionism from the doldrums and, ultimately, capture opinion throughout the Empire for a great imperial cause.

Chamberlain and tariff reform

For many years Chamberlain had been privately dubious about the wisdom of the United Kingdom's policy of free trade in a world that was increasingly turning to economic protection. It was not, it should be emphasised, that he was personally a protectionist in outlook. On the contrary, he hoped that international free trade could be restored. For the time being, however, he had come to the conclusion that British industry demanded protection in order to give it a breathing space from the cheap imports of government-subsidised producers abroad. The money raised from import tariffs, he believed, could be used to fund social reforms, as well as to assist the modernisation of British industry.

Such a policy was politically dangerous. Taxing imports meant a certain rise in food prices, since so much of the food consumed in Britain came from overseas; this in turn meant:

- it would be difficult to sell the idea to the working classes
- it would unite the Liberals in ferocious opposition
- it risked dividing the Unionists.

On the other hand, it offered almost the last chance for developing **imperial unification** as imperial trade could be exempted from taxation or subjected to reduced rates under an imperial preference tariff system.

Imperial unification
Bringing the 'mother' country (Britain) into closer economic and political unity with dominions and colonies.

Key question
What was the reaction to the idea of tariff reform?

Division over tariff reform

Whatever the risks, Chamberlain was not the man to shirk a challenge when such a prize was at stake. As early as May 1902 he hinted at the idea of an imperial trading system in a speech in his political stronghold, Birmingham. The government had just been forced to introduce a small tariff on imported corn to help pay for the costs of the Boer War and had been censured for doing so. In defending this tariff, Chamberlain hoped to undermine the inviolability of free trade, which he saw as outdated.

This speech occurred just before a Colonial Conference at which Chamberlain failed to convince the visiting Prime Ministers of the case for greater imperial integration. In the autumn of 1902 he left on a tour of South Africa that turned out to be a considerable success. Returning in early 1903 Chamberlain prepared himself for the launching of his great crusade. In May 1903, once more in Birmingham, he made a momentous speech that unquestionably changed the course of politics in the years up to the First World War. He declared himself in favour of an imperial preference tariff system designed to bring about an economic integration of the Empire. This speech initiated a debate that split the Unionists as a whole, with both the Conservatives and Liberal Unionists groups internally divided over their response.

Balfour attempted to preserve unity by adopting a fence-sitting strategy: he did not wish to break with Chamberlain and his supporters (who now, after all, included mainstream Conservatives) but, on the other hand, he was personally unconvinced of the case for 'tariff reform'. In any case, his main priority was party unity. While Balfour was using all his political skills (which were not inconsiderable) to keep the Unionists together, the opposing groups were formalising their positions:

- Chamberlain headed a Tariff Reform League set up in 1903.
- The free trade unionists formed the Unionist Free Food League in the same year.
- Some Unionists, including the young Winston Churchill, decided to defect to the Liberals. The following cartoon reflects the nature of the opposition to the idea of abandoning the principle of free trade.

'Through the Birmingham Looking Glass', *Westminster Gazette*, 6 October 1903. In what ways does the cartoon present an unsympathetic view of the tariff reform campaign? How would a supporter of tariff reform have countered the charges made in the cartoon? How fully does the cartoon contribute to an understanding of the issues raised in the tariff reform campaign?

Key question
How did the eventual defeat of the Unionists come about?

Key dates

Balfour resigns and the king appoints the Liberal leader, Sir Henry Campbell-Bannerman, as Prime Minister: 1905

The Liberal Party wins a massive victory in the general election: 1906

Defeat of the Unionists

In September 1903, Chamberlain resigned from the government in order to carry on a full-time campaign for tariff reform in the country at large. Leading free traders in the Cabinet also resigned, including the Duke of Devonshire.

Balfour's weakened administration limped on unconvincingly until the end of 1905, when, following an unexpectedly good showing in a by-election Balfour decided to resign without asking for a general election. Balfour's decision was a reaction to the confused political situation. Chamberlain's campaign had gained considerable ground within the ranks of the Unionists, but it had stalled badly in the country. The trade unions were hostile and there was no evidence to suggest that Chamberlain was converting the nation as a whole to his grand vision. Thus the Unionists remained divided, with no real prospect of resolving their differences, while the Liberals had a clear and united opposition to tariff reform that seemed to be in tune with public opinion.

In these circumstances Balfour realised that to continue in office much longer, with a general election due no later than the summer of 1907, would be fatal. In November 1905, two of the Liberal leaders, Campbell-Bannerman and Lord Rosebery, crossed swords publicly over the issue of Irish Home Rule (see page 34), which Rosebery wished to renounce. Balfour hoped that, by forcing the Liberals to take office, he would expose their internal divisions (not the least of these being over who would actually lead a Liberal administration), and divert attention from the Unionists' own difficulties. The strategy failed. The Liberals were by no means as divided as they appeared. Rosebery had little or no personal support in the party and Campbell-Bannerman had no real difficulty in forming a government. He was then able to call a general election for January 1906 from a position of strength.

A new scandal in South Africa concerning the terrible conditions suffered by Chinese immigrant workers helped to complete the Liberal's campaign. 'Chinese slavery', as the press dubbed it, had little to do with Balfour's administration, but it helped reawaken the scandal of the 'concentration camps' into which Boer civilians had been herded in the recent war, and enabled the Liberals to portray the Unionists as exploiters of the workers.

The result was an election triumph for the Liberals on a totally unexpected scale. They won 400 seats; the Unionists were reduced to a mere 157, some two-thirds of whom were 'Chamberlainite' tariff reformers. Balfour himself lost his seat and suffered the indignity of having to fight a further contest at a by-election to get back into the House of Commons. The overall result meant that the Liberals had a clear majority of 130. With the support of the Irish and Labour contingents (see pages 35–7) this would rise to over 350. The Unionist catastrophe was complete and could scarcely have been more humiliating.

Summary diagram: The decline of the Unionists

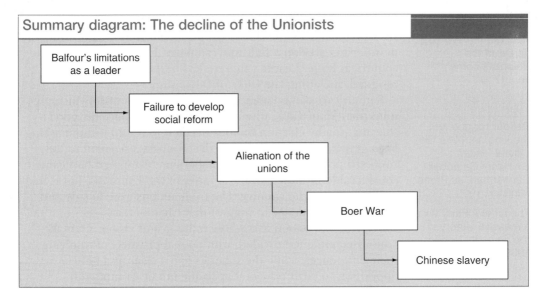

Balfour's limitations as a leader → Failure to develop social reform → Alienation of the unions → Boer War → Chinese slavery

Study Guide: AS Questions

In the style of AQA

Read the following source and then answer the questions that follow.

From: Frank McDonough, The British Empire 1815–1914, *1994.*

Before the [Boer] war the worst motive attributed to supporters of imperialism was excessive patriotism. Imperialism could even be seen as a 'positive mission' ... After the war this was no longer the case.

(a) Comment on 'positive mission' in the context of British imperialism at the end of the nineteenth century.   (3 marks)
(b) Explain in what ways the Boer War led to the end of 'splendid isolation' in British foreign policy.   (7 marks)

Exam tips
The cross-references are intended to take you straight to the material that will help you to answer the questions.

Effectively the source is only a stimulus and the questions probe your own knowledge.

(a) The key here is to make sure that your comments do reflect the context of Britain c. 1900. The 'positive mission' reflects, for example, the values of military power, the international prestige of Britain and the moral obligations of empire (pages 15–16).

(b) This assumes a causal link that many historians might dispute, or at least moderate, but you would be best advised to take it at face value for the purposes of the exam. The key points would be to refer to the problems the war created for Britain, such as the international isolation and condemnation of Britain's action and the exposure of military weaknesses in the early phase (page 18). You could link the particular concerns about the attitude of Germany to the desire for a better relationship with France (page 17).

In the style of OCR

How important was the Boer War (1899–1902) in the electoral defeat of the Conservatives in 1906?

Exam tips

The cross-references are intended to take you straight to the material that will help you to answer the question.

The key here is to recognise the evaluative aspect of the question. You are being asked to measure the extent of the importance of the specified factor (Boer War) in bringing about an event (electoral defeat). It follows that you will identify other factors that had an impact:

- the failure to deliver social reform (page 14)
- fear of increased food prices through tariff reform (page 21)
- concerns of the trade unions resulting from the Taff Vale case (pages 90–1).

You must decide how far these factors – jointly or individually – outweigh the importance of the Boer War or whether the war outweighs them. However you decide, it is usually a mistake in this type of question to dismiss the lead factor of the question too quickly. Even if you conclude that the Boer War was only a marginal factor (and you would probably be right) you should still consider the ways in which it did contribute (pages 18–19):

- the unexpectedly high costs of the war (in terms of men and money)
- difficulty in defeating the Boers
- dubious morality of the means of securing victory, etc.

You should evaluate, with reasons, the relative importance of the various factors that you consider.

---

2 The Liberal Party and 'New Liberalism' 1895–1906

POINTS TO CONSIDER

The period 1895–1906 was a time of significant change and development for the Liberal Party. With the retirement of its greatest figure, Gladstone, in 1894 the Party entered a period of internal division and electoral decline.

The Liberals were crushed in two general elections in 1895 and 1900. However, by 1906 they had recovered dramatically to record their own electoral triumph, form one of the strongest governments in British political history and go on to dominate government into the First World War. This chapter looks at:

- The origins of the Party and how this created tensions and the potential for division
- The emergence of a New Liberalism
- The problems that developed over Party leadership
- The reasons for the 1906 general election triumph.

Key dates

1859	Foundation of the modern Liberal Party
1886	Home Rule Bill for Ireland defeated in the House of Commons
1887	Joseph Chamberlain and the Liberal Unionists begin their collaboration with the Conservatives
1893	Home Rule is defeated in the House of Lords
1894	Gladstone resigns
	Lord Rosebery becomes new Prime Minister
1895	Liberals are heavily defeated in the general election by an alliance of Conservatives and Liberal Unionists.
1900	Conservative or 'Unionist' domination is continued in the so-called 'Khaki' election
1905	Prime Minister Balfour resigns
	The Liberal leader, Sir Henry Campbell-Bannerman, becomes Prime Minister
1906	The Liberal Party wins the general election by a massive majority

Key question
How did the Liberal Party come to be an established force in British politics in the nineteenth century?

1 | The Origins of the Liberal Party

The Liberal Party in 1895 was a broad-based **coalition** of diverse groups that had formally come together as the 'Liberal Party' in 1859. Because the Party had such diverse origins there was no detailed set of principles that could be said to make up 'liberalism'.

Indeed the lack of a very precise ideology was almost a necessity given the scope of views that the party needed to accommodate. The Liberal Party was formed in 1859 as a result of public interest in the issue of the unification of Italy, which had been taking shape during the 1850s in opposition to domination by the Austrian Empire. The Conservatives were broadly opposed to national movements threatening the status quo in Europe.

At this time, nationalists seeking freedom from the imperial powers of Austria, Russia and Turkey attracted support from 'liberals' all over Europe. This was because those imperial powers were **autocracies** without any form of representative government accountable to the people – or at least a part of the people. In 1859 as the movement for Italian unification entered a crucial phase, liberals in Britain decided to come together to express their support for a government that would in turn support the cause of Italian nationalists.

The five groups that came together to form the Liberal Party were the whigs, the Peelites, Independent Radicals, the Nonconformists and the Chartists.

The 'Whig' Party
This had been the dominant party of government since the **Great Reform Act** of 1832. Although seen generally as more **progressive** in attitude than the Conservatives, its leadership contained many aristocratic elements drawn from some of the oldest families in the country. So although it had been associated with important reforms in the past it was nevertheless basically traditional and even 'conservative' in outlook.

The 'Peelites'
The Peelites were supporters of Sir Robert Peel, who had headed a great Conservative Reforming Ministry from 1841 to 1846. Peel had reduced taxes on imports and exports drastically and had introduced the first peacetime income tax. Finally in 1846 he introduced the repeal of the **Corn Laws** that protected domestic farmers from foreign competition. These policies had led to a split in the Conservative Party that caused Peel's government to fall after the passing of the repeal of the Corn Laws. Peel died in 1850, but his supporters continued to maintain a separate identity. The most important of the Peelites was Gladstone, who was to become the most important single influence on the development of the Party up to 1895.

Key terms

Coalition
A coming together of different groups or political parties. Many countries are governed by coalition governments but it is unusual in Britain.

Autocracy
A system where one person has absolute rule.

Great Reform Act
An act that set standard voting qualifications in rural and urban constituencies, increasing numbers of votes from around 450,000 to 500,000.

Progressive
Prepared to introduce reform.

Corn Laws
Laws originally introduced in 1815 to tax cereal products coming into the country in order to protect domestic farmers from foreign competition.

The 'Independent Radicals'

This was a very loosely co-operating group with no real structure
or agenda. Essentially it was a group of individuals, with a very
general set of radical ideas. They did not always agree about
specific issues or about supporting the government of the day.
Their identity as a group was mainly based on the fact that they
did not fit with the other main parties.

The 'Nonconformists'

Nonconformists were members of those Churches that were
protestant but not prepared to accept the control of the Anglican
Church. They broadly supported Whigs or Radicals in elections
because they were less identified with maintaining the privileges
of the Anglican Church as the 'established' or state Church. There
were a great many of them in Scotland, Wales and parts of the
Midlands, although they were to be found all over the country in
lesser numbers. Nonconformists belonged to different Churches
and did not agree with each other on all issues, although all they
tended to be highly critical of Roman Catholicism. Nor were they
exclusively anti-Conservative. In particular, in some areas, the
Presbyterians, who were exceptionally anti-Roman Catholic, were
also very strong supporters of the Conservatives.

The 'Chartists'

The Chartists were a radical group of the 1830s and 1840s that
campaigned for working-class political rights. They took their
name from the 'People's Charter' of 1839, which set out their
demands. Although largely led by middle-class radicals, they
attracted the active support of more educated younger elements
among the working classes. Chartism collapsed as a national
movement at the end of the 1840s but historians have always
stressed that the real strength of Chartism lay in its local
organisations. More recently historians have increasingly argued
that Chartist identity did remain a factor in politics, especially at
local level, well beyond the period of its zenith. Eventually many
Chartists gravitated towards the Liberal Party.

The sheer diversity of the groups that made up the Liberal Party
meant that the leaders had to tread a very careful path if they
were not to end up offending one or other group. The clearest
example of this was to be the issue of Irish Home Rule,
championed by Gladstone in the 1880s. This policy upset some of
the aristocratic Whigs who sympathised with the Anglican
landowners in Ireland and radical Nonconformists who resented
concessions to Roman Catholics.

Key question
What were the factors behind the emergence of New Liberalism?

Key term

Old Whig
Those Liberals who had originally been part of the Whig Party, itself of aristocratic background.

William Gladstone

2 | New Liberalism

New Liberalism arose out of radical opposition to the direction that the Liberal Party was taking in the 1880s. The radicals in the Liberal Party had always disliked the aristocratic nature of most of the leadership. By the 1880s most of the **Old Whigs** were dead and the new generation lacked real commitment to radical reform. Even Gladstone, who had been seen by many as the radicals' main hope in the 1860s, was clearly not a radical when it came to social reform.

Gladstone's beliefs

Gladstone basically believed that progress was achieved by self-improvement and individual effort. He did not believe that governments should intervene directly to help individuals by such methods as providing state pensions for the elderly or helping children from poorer families.

Gladstone's political philosophy emphasised the personal responsibility of the individual. Gladstone beliefs can be summed up as follows:

- Individuals should be allowed as much personal freedom as possible.
- Business and the economic sector generally should be free from government interference and face the minimum of taxation burdens.
- The government should only intervene where there was a clear moral principle to be defended or promoted. For example, he came to accept that employers had responsibilities towards those they employed, especially women and children.
- Artificial barriers against self-improvement – for example social barriers – needed to be removed so that people of 'merit' could rise by their own efforts.

These ideas were essentially very conservative, 'Peelite' principles.

Gladstone became more liberal, as he grew older, on issues such as the right to vote and greater toleration of religious differences. However, even on these matters there was a limit to his liberalism. It never occurred to Gladstone, for example, that all men might have an inherent right to vote – he assumed that this right had to be earned by demonstrating virtues of education and civilised behaviour.

When it came to religion, Gladstone did gradually accept that other Christian denominations than the Anglican Church should have rights and should not be discriminated against. However, he still believed that the Anglican Church was morally superior and only agreed very reluctantly in the 1870s to accept the idea that non-Anglicans should be allowed into teaching posts at Oxford and Cambridge Universities, from which they had previously been barred by the universities' regulations.

But, while he was prepared to introduce limited reforms on these issues, he remained very suspicious of any idea that the state should intervene directly in areas he saw as personal or family responsibilities. For example, he hated the idea of compulsory state education and was suspicious even of any state involvement in education, although he at times agreed to reforms in education at the prompting of his Cabinet colleagues.

The Unauthorised Programme

Gladstone's conservatism on social issues was frustrating for those liberals who had more radical instincts. In 1885, the leading radical, Joseph Chamberlain (see profile in Chapter 1, pages 12–13), decided to address the issue head on by presenting his own set of proposals for a future Liberal Government to introduce:

- The abolition of all school fees for elementary education.
- Compulsory land purchase to create allotments and smallholdings for the rural lower classes.
- A graduated property tax so that government could impose higher taxes on the rich to pay for government spending.
- Reform of the House of Lords and shorter parliaments (three years maximum instead of seven), to make government more accountable.
- **Disestablishment** of the Church of England to put it on the same legal basis as other Churches.

This set of proposals became known as the 'Unauthorised Programme' because it was not the official policy of the Liberal Party. Gladstone did not approve of it, but as he could see the potential popularity of the ideas with lower class voters he did not openly condemn it. The Unauthorised Programme brought together ideas that had been discussed in radical circles for some time and in many ways represented the start of the clear challenge of 'New Liberalism' to the conservatism of Gladstone and his supporters.

Disestablishment The principle of separating the Church of England from its legal connection with the Constitution. *Key term*

The Newcastle Programme

In 1886 the clash in the Party over Home Rule for Ireland resulted in Chamberlain leaving the Liberals. However, not all radicals were prepared to take this extreme step and, in 1891, with an election looming, Gladstone was forced to accept a Liberal manifesto that offered a wider range of reforms than he would have liked in order to ensure party unity.

The manifesto became known as the 'Newcastle Programme' because Gladstone announced it in a speech in Newcastle upon Tyne. The Programme was hastily put together but bore the clear imprint of 'New Liberal' influence:

Home Rule bill for Ireland defeated in the House of Commons: 1886 *Key date*

- Home Rule was top of the agenda – at Gladstone's insistence.
- Compulsory land purchase for allotments as in the Unauthorised Programme (the end of school fees had already been brought in by the Conservatives in 1891).
- Tougher regulations controlling health and safety in the workplace.
- Greater employer liability for accidents at work.
- More limitations on the length of the working day.

- There were also references to greater democracy – 'one man, one vote', reform of the House of Lords, more democratic local government and payment for MPs to allow access to the House of Commons for a wider social range.

Gladstone accepted the package mainly because he had no intention whatsoever of putting it into effect. His principal concern was to achieve Home Rule for Ireland. He was 82. He intended to secure Home Rule and then retire immediately. He had no sympathy with the ideas behind the Newcastle Programme at all.

Beyond these kinds of ideas, however, 'New Liberalism' was breaking into areas that were the stuff of nightmares for Gladstone. The following policy ideas were all being discussed as remedies for the social problems that were increasingly evident:

- Pensions for the elderly.
- State-funded sickness benefits for those suffering from illness or injury.
- A national unemployment scheme.
- Payments to help working-class families support their children.

The adoption of similar schemes in Germany in the 1880s only served to increase the sense of urgency. In addition the so-called 'Socialist Revival' of the 1880s (see page 87) saw various groups spring into existence championing the cause of the working classes. These groups insisted that working-class interests could never be properly advanced through the Liberal Party, with its connections to the upper classes and the world of business and commerce.

For the New Liberals the emergence of groups that aimed to win over the increasing numbers of male working-class voters meant that there was an urgent need to show that the Liberals could in fact offer a meaningful package of reform proposals to address working-class interests.

Summary diagram: What was Liberalism?

Traditional Liberalism

- Minimum government intervention
- Strict control of government spending
- Minimum taxation
- Emphasis on individual responsibility

New Liberalism

- Greater government intervention
- Increased government spending on social reform
- Increased personal taxation for the wealthier classes
- More emphasis on collective responsibility

3 | The Leadership Question

Key question
How serious was the problem of the leadership succession?

When Gladstone finally retired as Prime Minister and Leader of the Liberal Party in 1894, there was no clear successor commanding universal support in the party. Gladstone had been such an awesomely dominant leader that it had seemed almost impertinent to many in the party to appear to be positioning to replace him.

In the 1880s the radical Joseph Chamberlain had been the most prominent of the Liberal leaders apart from Gladstone himself. However, Chamberlain had as many enemies as friends within the party and his disagreement with the 'Grand Old Man' over Irish Home Rule had led him to quit the party with a group of 'Liberal Unionists'. By 1894 this group had all but merged with the Conservatives and the following year joined them in a coalition government in which Chamberlain became Colonial Secretary and the acknowledged number two to the Prime Minister, Lord Salisbury. This left a group of younger Liberals vying to emerge as the successor to Gladstone.

Key dates
Joseph Chamberlain and the Liberal Unionists begin their collaboration with the Conservatives: 1887

Gladstone resigns: 1894

Lord Rosebery becomes Prime Minister: 1894

Liberals are heavily defeated in the General Election by an alliance of Conservatives and Liberal Unionists: 1895

Lord Rosebery

In terms of social status he was the most prominent figure in the Party. He was also intellectually brilliant and an expert on foreign policy. He had been Foreign Secretary under Gladstone and succeeded him as Prime Minister in 1894. Despite this, and the fact that he was still relatively young at 47, he was not by any means certain to be the long-term successor. His interest in politics was erratic and he was a leader who intended to lead very much on his own terms. After the election victory of the Conservatives (Unionists) in 1895 he became less active in his participation in the debates in the House of Lords. In 1896 he announced that he was resigning the leadership of the party. As a peer, he was not much favoured by the radical wing of the party in the House of Commons. He could also be extremely difficult to work with in government. Even so Rosebery remained a prominent figure and refused to rule out a comeback.

Herbert Henry Asquith

Asquith was widely regarded as one of the more radical of the leading figures. He was a prominent barrister and one of the most gifted of the younger Liberals. His marriage into an aristocratic family had given him useful social connections. He came from Yorkshire rather than the Home Counties and from a Nonconformist background, which made him popular with the radicals. Barely 40 years old when Gladstone made him Home Secretary in 1892, Asquith looked certain to be leader eventually. However, Asquith had an expensive wife and could not afford to give up his high earnings as a barrister for full-time political activity unless he had the cushion of a ministerial salary and expenses, so for the time being he was prepared to wait.

Sir William Harcourt

Harcourt was Gladstone's Chancellor of the Exchequer and he led the Party following Rosebery's resignation. In many ways he was the most natural successor to Gladstone. He was a veteran politician, 67 years old in 1894, and easily the most experienced of Gladstone's colleagues. His views were very much in line with those of the great man. Harcourt was widely respected as a formidable performer in the House of Commons. However, he disliked party intrigues and was not well suited to inspiring unity in a party that was made up of so many factions, who could all so easily end up fighting each other rather than the opposition. He was also undermined by Rosebery, who, though he himself did not wish to lead, was resentful towards those who did. Harcourt resigned in 1898, and retired from active politics, fed up with the in-fighting and divisions in the party.

Sir Edward Grey

Grey was even younger than Asquith, only 32 at the time of Gladstone's retirement in 1894. Even so he had staked a claim to be considered as a future leader. He had been Rosebery's second in command at the Foreign Office and, with the Foreign Secretary in the House of Lords, had had to take the lead on foreign policy matters on behalf of the government in the House of Commons. He had done very well in this role. He was, however, a close associate of Asquith and was unlikely to contest the leadership with him.

Sir Henry Campbell-Bannerman

Campbell-Bannerman was, apart from Harcourt, the oldest and most experienced of the Liberal leaders. He was Gladstone's Secretary of State for War (what would now be termed Defence Secretary) and had previously been Irish Secretary. When Harcourt resigned in 1898 the leadership fell to Campbell-Bannerman almost automatically. He was already 62 by then and not in the best of health. He was a Liberal who had, unusually, become more radical as he had grown older. He did not command wide enthusiasm in the party but equally he had no real enemies or groups opposed to him. His age and poor health meant that he was no threat in the long term to the younger contenders. In many ways therefore he was the ideal leader for the time being.

To outsiders, the continually changing leadership and the lack of a really dominating successor to Gladstone seemed to suggest a party with a leadership crisis. In reality however the situation was less critical than it appeared. By 1900 all the main figures of the Party, apart from Rosebery, had accepted Campbell-Bannerman's leadership. To outsiders, Rosebery, as a former Prime Minister and still relatively young man, seemed to be still a formidable figure, but within the Party most people had lost patience with his posturing, inconsistencies and selfish manner. The younger potential leaders, most critically Asquith, were content, for a variety of reasons, to bide their time. Most important of all, the leading Liberals were well aware that they could not afford to allow disputes over the leadership to affect their ability to form a government if the opportunity ever arose.

Summary diagram: Liberal leaders

1868–75	William Gladstone
1875–80	Lord Granville (Lords) and Lord Hartington (Commons)*†
1880–94	William Gladstone
1894–6	Lord Roseberg
1896–8	Sir William Harcourt
1898–1906	Sir Henry Campbell-Bannerman

*Lord Hartington was not a peer but an MP. His father was the Duke of Devonshire. It was, and still is, usual for the sons of peers to use any lesser title of the family – in this case 'Marquis of Hartington'.

†It was not unusual for there to be separate leaders of a party in the Commons and Lords when a party was in opposition.

---

4 | The General Election of 1906

On 4 December 1905 Arthur Balfour resigned as Prime Minister and brought to an end the coalition government of Conservatives and Liberal Unionists that had held power since 1895. Balfour refused, however, to advise the king to dissolve Parliament and hold a general election. Constitutionally this meant that the king had to send for the official Liberal leader, Sir Henry Campbell-Bannerman, and invite him to form a new government. This was part of Balfour's strategy. He hoped to provoke a crisis in the Liberal Party that would weaken it and allow him, eventually, to win another general election for the Unionists. Why did Balfour resort to such a complicated strategy?

- Campbell-Bannerman and the former Prime Minister, Lord Rosebery, had clashed publicly in November 1905 over the issue of Irish Home Rule. Rosebery wanted to abandon it as a Liberal policy – Campbell-Bannerman intended to retain it.
- Campbell-Bannerman's position as leader appeared insecure. Asquith and Sir Edward Grey were possible alternatives, as was Lord Rosebery himself. Although they had accepted his leadership in opposition, Balfour was by no means certain that they would do so in government. There was a doubt therefore as to whether Campbell-Bannerman would actually be able to form a government, especially since it was known that his

Key question
How did the Liberal Party achieve its landslide victory of 1906?

Key dates

Prime Minister Balfour resigns: 1905

The Liberal leader, Sir Henry Campbell-Bannerman, becomes Prime Minister: 1905

The Liberal Party wins the general election by a massive majority: 1906

health was fragile. If the Liberals failed in the attempt, the
Unionist position would be massively strengthened.
- The Unionists had been, according to all the political
commentators of the day, heading for a serious defeat at the
next election, which would have to be held, at the latest, by the
middle of 1907. They had however done better than expected
in two by-elections in November 1905. This encouraged
Balfour to think that perhaps the tide had turned and a bold
strike to undermine the Liberals' credibility might swing
electoral opinion back towards the Unionists.

The Liberals form government

Balfour's strategy was too subtle for its own good, however. The
Liberals were by no means as divided as they had appeared.
Campbell-Bannerman had no real problems forming a
government. Neither Asquith nor Grey was prepared to put at
risk the chance of holding high office, especially when 'C-B' was
over 70 and not in good health. Asquith accepted the position of
Chancellor of the Exchequer and Grey became Foreign Secretary.
Lord Rosebery had little or no personal support by now in the
Liberal Party and his eventual refusal to serve in the Liberal
Government was no surprise. Once the government was formed,
Campbell-Bannerman immediately asked the king to dissolve
Parliament so that a general election could be held in January
1906. The result was a landslide victory for the Liberals of epic
proportions. The Unionist dominance was totally overturned
(see Table 2.1).

Table 2.1: Seats in the House of Commons after the 1900 and 1906
elections

1900		1906	
Unionists	402	Unionists	157
Liberals	186	Liberals	400
LRC/Labour	2	LRC/Labour	52*
Irish National Party	82	Irish National Party	83

* Made up of 29 Labour Representation Committee (LRC) MPs who
were joined by 21 Miners' Union MPs and two Independent Labour
MPs after the election to form the Labour Party.

The defeat of the Unionists

Key question
'Why did the
Unionists suffer
such a humiliating
defeat?

There is no single factor to explain the catastrophe that befell the
Unionists in 1906. Instead, a number of factors worked together
to undermine them both internally and how they appeared to the
electorate:

- The Unionists had become seen as the party of imperialism.
This, after the scandal of the Boer War 'concentration camps'
(see pages 18–19), was a liability rather than an asset.
- The Unionists were seriously divided over economic policy.
Some supported the continuance of free trade, while others
increasingly wanted to adopt a system of protective tariffs as

advocated by Joseph Chamberlain. Many historians see this as a critical factor because abandoning free trade meant taxing food imports, which would put up food prices.

- The Education Act of 1902 (see pages 10–14) had reunited many Nonconformist voters behind the Liberals.
- Trade unionists were particularly active and well organised – some in support of the Liberals and some in support of the Labour Representation Committee (LRC) – because of the 1901 Taff Vale case (see Chapter 5, pages 90–1).
- The Unionists had failed, despite much discussion, to produce social reform legislation in key areas, such as child welfare, unemployment and sickness benefits and old age pensions.
- Balfour, despite being a superb analyst with considerable intellectual and administrative skills, was a poor leader. He had little feel for mass issues and could be very indecisive, for example, over the issue of protective tariffs where he failed to give a clear lead.
- In 1903 the Liberals agreed on a secret 'electoral pact' with the LRC. Under its terms the Liberals agreed not to put up candidates in some seats where the LRC had the better chance of winning. The LRC agreed to reciprocate in other seats where the Liberals were stronger. The arrangements centred on those constituencies where the Unionists might possibly win the seat in the event of a split vote between the Liberals and the LRC. It was not a binding commitment and it worked through an informal, personal agreement reached by Herbert Gladstone for the Liberals, and Ramsay MacDonald for the LRC. Even so, this arrangement enabled the LRC to achieve its electoral breakthrough and also secured a number of otherwise **marginal seats** for the Liberals.
- Finally, a scandal erupted in South Africa over the terrible working conditions being endured by Chinese contract workers in the South African mines. The scandal, described as 'Chinese slavery' by the press, reinforced the image of the Unionists as the uncaring party of worker exploitation, even though, in reality, they had no responsibility for, or ability to change, the conditions of the Chinese workers.

The result of these factors, taken together, was catastrophic for the Unionists. Balfour lost his seat at the election and was forced into fighting a by-election later in the year before he could return to the House of Commons. Two-thirds of the remaining Unionist MPs were Chamberlain supporters who wanted to abandon free trade, while the other third were pledged to retain it. The Liberals had an overall majority of 108 but were likely to be supported in most things by both the **Irish Nationalists** and the Labour Party. This meant they were now capable of amassing immense majorities (over 350) in the House of Commons where, for the time being at least, the Unionists were now almost an irrelevance.

Key terms

Marginal seat
Constituency where the MP has only a small majority and there is a real possibility of its being won by another MP from a different party.

Irish Nationalists
Those Irish politicians who demanded greater (or even full) independence for Ireland from Great Britain.

Summary diagram: The general election 1906

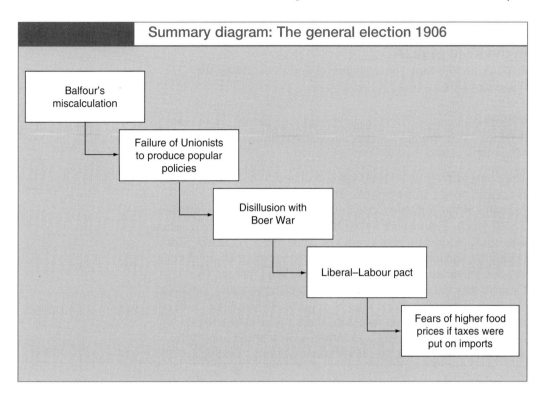

Study Guide: AS Questions

In the style of AQA

1 Read the following source material and then answer the questions that follow.

Source A

Adapted from: Stephen J. Lee, Aspects of British Political History 1815–1914, *1994.*

The conservatives after 1900 were accused of not caring about the social needs of the people. They were criticised for their handling of the Taff Vale Case and the 'Chinese Slavery' affair in South Africa. Even where Prime Minister Balfour made a positive attempt to address a major national issue in his Education Act (1902), he succeeded in stirring up … Nonconformist opinion, which committed itself wholeheartedly to the Liberals. The Liberals themselves launched attacks on Conservative initiatives like the Education Act and Chamberlain's proposals for tariff reform. The latter helped re-create the traditional free trade beliefs of the Liberal party and to focus on a bread and butter issue which was bound to attract more working-class votes.

Source B

Adapted from: Malcolm Pearce and Geoffrey Stewart, British Political History, 1867–1990, *1992.*

If Balfour tried to tackle Britain's problems one by one, Joseph Chamberlain produced a sweeping solution … , which was to split the Tory Party and halt Conservative domination. On 15 May 1903, Chamberlain declared his faith in 'imperial preference' in a famous speech at Birmingham. He proposed to abandon free trade, a principle of British life for fifty years. A system of duties, lower for goods within the Empire, would tie the Empire together, raise revenue for social reform and protect British industry. The tariff reform campaign had been launched.

Source C

Adapted from: the speech made by Joseph Chamberlain in Birmingham on 15 May 1903.

I believe in a British Empire which should be self-sufficient and able to maintain itself against the competition of all rivals, although it should be one of its first duties to cultivate friendship with all the nations of the world. And I do not believe in a little England which shall be separated from lands to which it should in the natural course look to for support and affection – a little England which would be at the mercy of those who envy its present prosperity.

(a) Use Source A and your own knowledge.
Explain briefly what was meant by the 1902 'Education Act' in the context of political controversy at the time. (3 marks)

(b) Use Source C and your own knowledge.
How useful is Source C as evidence of Joseph Chamberlain's reasons for launching his 'tariff reform' campaign? (7 marks)

(c) Use Sources A, B and C and your own knowledge.
'Joseph Chamberlain's tariff reform campaign was to blame for the Conservatives' loss of the 1906 General Election.' Explain why you agree or disagree with this statement. (15 marks)

Source: AQA, June 2003

Exam tips

The cross-references are intended to take you straight to the material that will help you to answer the questions.

(a) The focus here needs to be on why the Act was controversial. The source itself gives you a clue by referring to the Nonconformist opposition. It is usually a good idea to read the source carefully in this type of question as it often does give help of this kind. Here the key idea is to write about why the Nonconformists opposed the Act rather than what it contained in general. So you should focus on the requirement in the Act that the newly created LEAs should provide support for the Anglican 'voluntary' schools out of the local rates. This outraged Nonconformists and led the Liberal Party, who traditionally drew considerable support from Nonconformist voters, to oppose the measure in Parliament (page 11).

(b) The key here is to concentrate on what the source says and who is generating it and in what context.

- The source shows that the campaign is linked to Chamberlain's perception of the future of the Empire – Chamberlain himself is the originator of the source (an obvious point but no relevant point is too obvious to make in this type of question). Chamberlain was a 'New Imperialist' and the source is a useful piece of evidence showing his thinking on this issue.
- Then use your own knowledge to set the context – Chamberlain has tried for some time previously to convince the Cabinet to adopt his idea for tariff reform and failed; now he has resigned from the government to campaign publicly (pages 21–2).

Always look on the positive side of sources in this type of question – if there are negative points you feel you can legitimately make, well and good, but never let them predominate in your answer.

(c) To get the top level of marks in this question you need to offer a clear judgement about the statement. It must be a balanced judgement showing that you understand that there is evidence both ways, but don't sit on the fence with your answer. Be specific about the arguments.

- Show why it could be argued that the statement is correct, such as concern about food prices and divisions in the Conservatives ranks over the issue (pages 21–3).
- However, also consider a range of other factors – failure to deliver social reform, etc. (pages 35–6).

Plan an answer like this.

- You need to decide *before* you start whether you agree or not.
- Make sure that you refer to all three sources in the course of the answer.
  - Source A gives important information about factors other than tariff reform that played a part in the election defeat of the Conservatives.
  - Sources B and C deal directly with the principles of tariff reform itself.
- Expand on these points from your own knowledge and try to draw in relevant information not offered by the sources themselves.
- Your argument is best made clear from the outset, and sustained throughout your answer, by making a specific comment about each piece of evidence as you refer to it. Avoid the type of answer that lists all the relevant factors in turn and then ends by saying 'As can be seen from the above the statement is true overall'.

2 Read the following source and then answer the questions that follow.

Adapted from: Malcolm Pearce and Geoffrey Stewart, British Political History 1867–1990, *1992.*

The Election in January 1906 was a Unionist [Conservative] nightmare. It was certainly a landslide for the Liberals. Now 400 Liberals faced 157 Unionists. The Labour Party won 30 seats.

(a) Using the source and your own knowledge, comment on 'landside' in the context of the 1906 General Election.

(3 marks)

(b) Explain why the Labour Party won 30 seats. (7 marks)

(c) 'The Conservatives' record in government between 1900 and 1905 made it likely that they would lose the General Election in 1906.'

Explain why you agree or disagree with this statement.

(15 marks)

Source: AQA, June 2001

Exam tips

The cross-references are intended to take you straight to the material that will help you to answer the questions.

(a) The term 'landslide' refers to an overwhelming victory.
  - Use the figures in the source to show how complete was the victory of the Liberals.
  - Use your own knowledge to point out that the Labour Party could be expected generally to support the Liberals (election pact) increasing their majority still further (page 36).
  - Additionally there were over 80 Irish Nationalist MPs also likely to support the Liberals because of their support for Home Rule (page 36).

(b) Strictly use your own knowledge here and you must do more than list reasons to gain high marks. The key is to explain clearly why the reasons are relevant. So the most important point here is the electoral pact with the Liberals and you need to show how it worked to increase the chances of Labour candidates being elected in certain constituencies (page 36). Also you could refer to increased trade union support, but show how they supported Labour with considerable funds to finance the election campaign (page 36).

(c) You must interpret 'record in government' widely so as to include what they did not do as well as their actual actions. Lack of social reforms will be a major issue and you need to show what specific problems they might have addressed in order to show why it was a factor (pages 8–14). By all means bring in issues like 'Chinese slavery', where the government was not in fact responsible at all for the situation in South Africa, but where they were nevertheless perceived to be guilty (page 23). The basic issues such as Taff Vale and tariff reform need some development to show why they had an adverse effect on the government chances of winning in 1906 (pages 90–1).

In the style of OCR

'Tariff reform was the most important factor in the Liberal election victory of 1906'. How far do you agree with this view?

Exam tips

The cross-references are intended to take you straight to the material that will help you to answer the question.

This wording indicates an evaluative approach – treat it the same as a 'To what extent' or 'How important' style of wording. You need to examine all the ways in which the campaign for tariff reform helped the Liberals (pages 21–3), for example:

- It united them in defence of free trade.
- It divided the Conservatives into those who supported it and those who preferred to keep free trade.
- It caused some Conservatives to switch sides to the Liberals, e.g. Churchill.
- It raised fears among the working-class voters that there would be higher food prices.
- It divided manufacturers into those who saw the benefits of protection and those who feared increased costs and reduced exports.

Part of the assessment however needs to involve how great a part the issue played in the election victory, so you need to balance your answer by showing awareness of these wider factors, for example:

- The failure of the Conservatives to address demands for social reform (page 14).
- The concerns of the trade unions over the right to strike without the risk of being sued (page 67).
- The moral issues raised by the Boer War (pages 18–19).
- The 'Chinese slavery' scandal (page 23).

To score highly with this kind of essay question it is crucial that you are seen to be offering clear judgements all the way through your answer. Make sure that you always support your judgements with factual evidence and that they are balanced to take account of all the possible different interpretations.

Set out your view at the start and work the answer towards supporting it – to do this you must plan your answer and follow the plan. Never use an essay of this kind to make up your mind what you think; that is the purpose of planning – decide then execute.

3

The Liberals and Social Reform 1906–14

POINTS TO CONSIDER
Social conditions relate to the standard of living enjoyed by a nation's people and in particular the standards of life of its poorest and most vulnerable inhabitants. Although by 1900 the poorest classes in Britain were undoubtedly better off than they had been in the past, there was concern about how fast conditions were improving and about the standards gap between the poor and the middle and upper classes, which seemed to be increasing. In this chapter the issue of social reform will be examined in three ways:

- The attitudes to social reform
- The Liberal reforms
- An assessment of the achievements of the Liberals.

Key dates

1906	Liberals win January general election
	The Education (Provision of Meals) Act
1906–8	Legislation to help children from poorer families
1907	Education Act
1908	Children's Act
	Old Age Pension Act
1909	Introduction of old age pensions
	The 'People's Budget' introduced, increasing taxes for the wealthy
1911	National Insurance Act

1 | Attitudes to Social Reform

Key question
Why was social reform a priority for the Liberals by 1906?

The failure to develop a policy of **social reform** to meet the needs of the lower classes was one of the main reasons for the decline in the position of the Unionist Government by 1905. The Liberals were determined not to make the same mistake and after they formed the government in 1905 they started a programme of social reform.

Key term

Social reform
The introduction of new laws to improve social conditions.

The reasons why social reform had become such an important issue were:

- the inadequacy of the existing provision for the poor
- the growing interest and studies into poverty by social reformers
- the Boer War.

The Poor Law and workhouses

In 1905 the main safety net provided by the state to protect people who lacked any means of support was the Poor Law (first created in 1601, but amended in 1834). This later amendment introduced the 'deterrent principle', which meant that people without any means of supporting themselves were discouraged from seeking aid unless there was absolutely no alternative. In order to achieve this, the workhouses, which were run on a strict regime of discipline, had been set up to accommodate anyone genuinely seeking support, but to deter those able-bodied men and women who were thought to be seeking help out of laziness, when really they were perfectly capable of working for a living.

In fairness to the founders of the system, the intention had never been to apply a harsh workhouse regime to defenceless people such as children, the elderly or even those unemployed men and women who were honestly seeking work. However, over the course of the nineteenth century, the nature of workhouses had changed. From being originally conceived of as short-term deterrents for scroungers, they had become the primary refuge of the old, the sick, and abandoned women and their children. These people overwhelmingly made up the bulk of the workhouse population by the 1880s. Even so the deterrent principle was still applied, though in varying degrees of severity from place to place.

The prison-like appearance and internal discipline of the workhouses made them an object of fear and shame for those most likely to end up in them. Many people routinely put up with severe deprivation rather than submit to entering a workhouse.

By the 1890s, the scandal of deprivation and the grimness of the workhouses had become demanding political issues. Both of the main political parties were, in theory, committed to do something about the situation. From the late 1860s onwards Conservative and Liberal Governments both introduced legislation aimed at improving the state of **public health** and controlling the worst conditions in factories and agricultural work. These policies, however, did nothing to address the core problem of the working classes – inadequate or inconsistent incomes (especially in old age or infirmity) and a lack of access to medical treatment.

Studies into poverty

From the 1880s a series of investigations undertaken by social reformers anxious to force the government to take action, revealed the extent of the poverty that many people were enduring.

Public health
A general term relating to issues such as disease, sanitation, living and working conditions and pollution.

Key term

In 1881 the publication of *Progress and Poverty* by an American, Henry George, sparked off the interest. Actual case studies of real families began to build up a picture of the standard of living of the poor. These studies showed conditions of overcrowding and substandard housing, malnutrition and ill health, and caused the political debate to develop and intensify. Two investigations stand out as particularly influential. These were:

- Charles Booth's *Life and Labour of the People of London* – a massive study published over the period 1889–1903 in several volumes.
- Seebohm Rowntree's *Poverty, A Study of Town Life*, which appeared in 1903.

Booth argued that 30 per cent of the population of London fell below a poverty line income level of between 90 and 105 pence per week. Rowntree's study was based on York and showed a similar picture. Rowntree also applied a very tight set of guidelines for defining poverty so as to avoid any charge of exaggeration of his findings. The overall message of these investigations was that around one-third of the entire population was living in conditions which were dangerously deprived.

Impact of the Boer War

In itself this evidence might still have not been enough to produce a political response. However, the Boer War of 1899–1902 produced an unexpected impetus for social reform. Britain did not have a system of **conscription** so when additional troops were needed for the war the army had to rely on those men who were willing to volunteer. There was no shortage of recruits, but an alarming percentage of those who did apply were found to be unfit for military service through a variety of medical conditions.

The Boer War was a relatively small conflict against an enemy that did not pose any direct threat, so the high rate of rejection of volunteers did not affect the army too badly. However, it raised the question of what might happen if Britain faced a much larger conflict in Europe at some point in the future. The health of the nation therefore took on quite a different aspect when seen in that way and some people who might not have sympathised with social reform purely for its own sake became convinced of its necessity.

Key term

Conscription
Compulsory military service.

The Liberal Party's attitude towards social reform

The Liberals took office in 1905 with a general commitment to the improvement of working-class conditions. However, though they were pledged to do this in general terms they took over the government with few really detailed proposals. This was partly due to the suddenness with which they came to power and the immediate need to call a general election (see pages 34–5). But, it also stemmed from the divisions they had suffered in recent years and the potentially controversial nature of any new social reform legislation.

Key question
Why was social reform a controversial subject?

- The enthusiasts for 'New Liberalism', such as David Lloyd George, wished to see the government intervening much more directly to help improve life for the lower classes. This meant introducing national schemes for unemployment benefits, sickness benefits, old age pensions and even the introduction of child allowances, all of which would have to be paid for mainly out of the taxes imposed on the better off.
- More traditional Liberals still clung to the idea of individual effort and enterprise as the means to self-improvement.

Although the leading Liberals, like the new Prime Minister, Sir Henry Campbell-Bannerman, and his Chancellor of the Exchequer, Herbert Asquith, mostly leaned towards intervention, they were only too aware of the need to move very cautiously in the interests of maintaining unity within the Liberal Party as a whole.

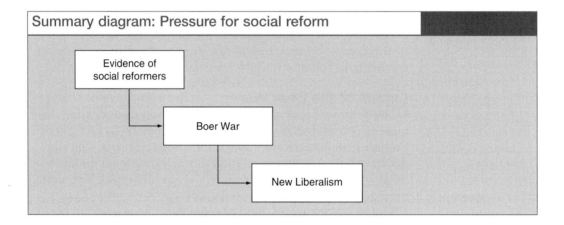

Summary diagram: Pressure for social reform

2 | The Liberal Reforms

The controversial nature of the question of how to go about improving the lives of the poorest sections of society meant that firm plans of action might have proved too divisive in the run-up to an election. However, when the Liberals won their great election victory in 1906 they were committed in principle to bringing in social reforms to benefit the lowest classes. Their attention centred on three areas:

Liberals win January general election: 1906

Key date

- the condition of children of the poorest families
- the condition of elderly people with no means of independent support
- the problem of poverty resulting from sickness and unemployment.

The welfare of children 1906–8

The least controversial of these areas was the question of the condition of working-class children. Children were not only the most directly vulnerable section of society, they were also the only group that could not be held in any way to blame for their

Key question
In what ways did working-class children need support?

problems. Sickness could be seen as self-inflicted or feigned and unemployment as the result of sheer laziness. Even the elderly could be seen as poverty-stricken in old age because of a lack of saving during their working lives. None of these accusations could reasonably be levelled at children. Those who wanted reform on a wider scale saw the cause of suffering children as a powerful emotional starting point.

Even so, some (including some Liberals) still believed that children were solely the concern of their parents or families and that any government intervention on their behalf would undermine individual freedom and individual responsibility. Despite such views, however, there was a general feeling that the pitiful condition of the poorest working-class children was nothing short of a national disgrace.

The Education (Provision of Meals) Act 1906

The first direct move to ease the suffering of deprived children came in 1906 with the passing of the Education (Provision of Meals) Act. The issue of undernourished children had increasingly been highlighted since the extension of local rate support to all schools in the 1890s and the creation of Local Education Authorities (LEAs) in the 1902 Education Act (see page 11).

The problem was that children who were too hungry and physically weak could not benefit properly from education. Reports from local doctors and school inspectors were well documented by 1906. The result was a **Private Member's Bill** introduced by a Labour MP, which the Liberal Government took over and adopted as government policy.

The 1906 Act enabled LEAs to provide school meals for 'needy' children by charging an additional rate of a halfpenny in the pound. However, the key word here was 'enabled'. The Act did not make it compulsory for LEAs to do this and many did not rush to take up their new power. By 1911 less than one-third of them were using additional rates to provide school meals and the Board of Education decided to take additional powers under which they could order such provision.

The Education Act 1907

In 1907, the Liberal Government introduced a new Education Act, which made school medical inspections for children compulsory. Under this Act:

- At least three inspections had to take place during a child's school years.
- These inspections were to be conducted in school and during school hours by a properly qualified doctor.
- The first inspection had to be done as soon as possible after the child had started school.

Unlike the regulations covering the provision of school meals this legislation was compulsory from the start. This was because:

Key term

Private Member's Bill
All MPs have a right to introduce bills on their own initiative, which, if passed, become law. In the nineteenth century it was very common for even major pieces of legislation to be sponsored in this way by individual MPs rather than the government and sometimes even in defiance of the government. This virtually died out during the twentieth century and the very few Private Member's Bills that are allowed in any session can only succeed with the government's agreement.

School Medical Officer (examining child's eyes). "Now, LITTLE GIRL, CAN YOU SEE MY FINGER?"
Child (coyly). "I SHAN'T TELL YOU."

Cartoon reflecting the compulsory school inspections for children

- Compulsory elements in laws concerning public health matters had been used in all kinds of situations since the first Public Health Act of 1848, so compulsion on this kind of issue was not very controversial.
- The recruitment of volunteers for the Boer War had produced a sense of urgency about improving the health of the young (see page 45). This was because it had shown just how appalling the health standards suffered by large numbers of the working-class population actually were.

The Children's Act 1908

In 1908, the Children's Act introduced a variety of measures to deal with wider aspects of neglect and abuse. **Juvenile courts** and **remand homes** were set up to remove child offenders from the adult courts and prisons. Severe penalties were introduced for the ill treatment of children, and also for selling them tobacco and alcohol in unsealed containers. Finally, in the budget of 1909, Lloyd George introduced direct financial assistance for child welfare in the form of child allowances to be paid at a rate of £10 per year per child for the poorest families.

These measures to improve the welfare of children were the Liberal's principal achievement during their first two years in office.

The Liberals failed in an attempt to introduce an eight-hour day for the mining industry. They did manage to ensure that the principle of Workmen's Compensation, for injuries occurring in the workplace, was extended to cover some six million workers, but overall, only the Child Welfare reforms stopped it from

Key terms

Juvenile courts
Law courts dealing only with offences committed by children.

Remand homes
Detention centres where children convicted of offences could be sent to learn and develop rather than being sent to prison.

seeming a very unimpressive record. Even allowing for the progress in helping working-class children to obtain a better start in life, some of the more radical Liberals, such as Lloyd George, were less than satisfied.

Asquith takes over

In April 1908, the Prime Minister Campbell-Bannerman was forced to resign through illness. Asquith was his natural successor (see page 32) and, in the Cabinet reshuffle that followed, Lloyd George, who had built up a formidable reputation at the Board of Trade, was promoted to become the Chancellor of the Exchequer. He was replaced at the Board of Trade by Winston Churchill.

Churchill was a former Conservative who had joined the Liberals in protest against the policy of tariff reform in 1903 (see page 22). He had since established himself as a radical reformer. Lloyd George and Churchill were determined to use their new seniority to push for a much more ambitious programme of social reform. Not only did they genuinely want more radical reforms, they also believed that it was a political necessity for the Liberals to show themselves capable of developing a really progressive policy if the party was not to lose out in future elections to the Unionists and the Labour Party.

Old age pensions

When the Liberals came to power in 1905 there was no provision for **state pensions** for the elderly. Old people were expected either to continue working to support themselves or to have saved enough in their working lives to maintain themselves in retirement. Failing either of these there was only the charity of their families or the workhouses provided under the feared and hated Poor Law. For most working-class people only the last two options really applied, as their incomes were too low for saving on the scale that would provide for old age, and their work was usually too physically demanding to be carried on in old age.

The basic principle that some kind of financial support should be provided by the state for a dignified old age had been discussed since the 1880s, but the cost of providing such a system had deterred successive governments from taking on the issue.

The Old Age Pension Act 1908

During the last phase of his time as Chancellor of the Exchequer, Asquith had been working on the idea of introducing a system of old age pensions. His budget proposals for 1908 contained provisions for financing the introduction of a scheme and Lloyd George inherited the responsibility for putting the finishing touches to the budget and presenting it to the House of Commons.

Lloyd George then took on the job of piloting an old age pensions bill through into law. The provision that this made for the poorest of the elderly was relatively modest, especially when considered against the length of time it had taken to get any form

Key question
Who benefited from the introduction of old age pensions?

Key term

State pension
Money paid to people over a certain age out of state funds.

Profile: David Lloyd George 1863–1945

1863	– Born
1890	– Elected MP
1906	– Cabinet minister as President of Board of Trade
1908	– Chancellor of the Exchequer
1908	– Introduced old age pensions
1909	– Introduced 'People's Budget'
1911	– Introduced unemployment and sickness benefits
1915	– Minister for Munitions
1916	– Secretary for War
1917	– Prime Minister
1922	– Forced to resign
1945	– Died

Background

David Lloyd George was born in Manchester in 1863. His father was a school headmaster who died very soon after his son's birth. Lloyd George's mother, left with no other means of support, returned to her home village of Llanystumdwy in North Wales to live with her brother, who ran a small business as a shoemaker. Lloyd George was therefore brought up in a Welsh-speaking environment in which English was very much a second language.

The family were religious Nonconformists, hostile to both the Anglicanism and social and political predominance of the local English-speaking gentry families. Lloyd George's background was not well off financially but, on the other hand, it was culturally rich. His 'Uncle Lloyd', effectively his adopted father, was a man of considerable intellect and very strong religious faith. Although of limited formal education, Uncle Lloyd was passionate about the value of education and determined to give his adopted family (Lloyd George had an elder brother and sister) the best possible start in life. Uncle Lloyd taught himself French in order to be able to improve the children's education, and saw Lloyd George and his older brother safely through legal studies and into careers as solicitors.

Early career

Lloyd George was devoted to the idea of a political career from his teens and, at the age of 26, after making a name for himself as a rising nationalist figure on local political issues, he was elected as Liberal MP for Carnarvon Boroughs. This was despite determined opposition from the Conservatives who had previously dominated the constituency. He continued to represent the constituency for the next 55 years.

In 1902–3 Lloyd George took a leading role in the Nonconformists' opposition to the Balfour Education Act (see page 11). In 1905, when the Liberals came to power, he became a junior member of Campbell-Bannerman's Cabinet as President of the Board of Trade. He at once showed his administrative ability with a range of reforming legislation and, in 1908, when Asquith became Prime Minister, he appointed Lloyd George to replace him as Chancellor of the Exchequer.

Chancellor

As Chancellor, Lloyd George oversaw the completion of the old age pension legislation and developed the Budget of 1909. During the constitutional crisis with the House of Lords (see pages 68–9), Lloyd George became the leading critic of the peers' resistance, first to the Budget and then to the Parliament Bill. In 1911 he introduced the first National Insurance legislation. By 1914 he had developed a close working relationship with Asquith and was seen as second or possibly third (behind Sir Edward Grey, the Foreign Secretary) in terms of seniority.

Later career

During the First World War, Lloyd George was first of all responsible for adapting the country's financial policies to meet the needs of a wartime economy. From 1915 he was successively Minister of Munitions, Secretary for War and then Prime Minister in 1916. His appointment as Premier caused a clash with Asquith, which had disastrous consequences for the future of the Liberal Party and from which it arguably never recovered (see page 136).

After the war, Lloyd George continued to lead a coalition government with the Conservatives until their backbenchers withdrew their support in October 1922, which forced him to resign. He never held office again. His private life was controversial, especially his relationships with women, and he became the first Prime Minister to live openly with a 'mistress' (who was 25 years his junior). Remarkably, though his lifestyle was well known, no public scandal ever came out during his lifetime. In 1944, with his health in serious decline, and knowing he could not possibly fight another election campaign after the war he reluctantly accepted a peerage in the hope of being able to contribute to the post-war debates on the peace settlement. However he died in February 1945 with the war still unfinished, without having taken his place in the Lords.

of assistance provided. The first payments were finally made on 6 January 1909. The terms of the Act were:

- Pensions of 5s (25p) per week would be paid to those aged 70 or over who had annual incomes of £21 or less.
- For those with annual incomes over £21 a sliding scale of reduced payments would be made. Those with an annual income of £31 or over would receive no payment.
- There were a number of categories of people excluded:
  - those who had claimed poor relief in the previous year
  - people who had been in prison in the previous 10 years
  - those who had failed to work regularly.

In practice these rules did not result in a great reduction in the number of claimants. The qualifying period for ex-convicts was eventually reduced to two years.

By 1914, there were 970,000 claimants, costing the Exchequer a total of £12 million a year.

Though often criticised for the relatively high starting age – 70 was a tougher milestone to achieve then than it has subsequently become – the system had a massive impact on the lives of the beneficiaries (see Table 3.1). The 'Lloyd George money', as it became widely known, released many from the threat of the workhouse or dependence on often hard-pressed relatives. A pensions system had been under discussion since the 1880s at least. The Liberals made it a reality.

Key date
Introduction of old age pensions: 1909

Table 3.1: Typical weekly living costs of an elderly person in 1908 as published in a radical magazine, *The Woman Worker*.

	s.	d.
Rent	2	3
Paraffin (pint)	1	½
Coal	2	½
Tea	1	
Sugar	1	½
Potatoes	1	
Mutton	1	0
Flour	1	
Porter (a type of beer)	1	¾
Pepper, salt and vinegar	1	½
Loaf of bread	2	½
Total:	4	5¼ (22p)

Key question
What is the value of this kind of evidence to a historian studying the introduction of old age pensions in 1909?

Comparing old and new money
Before 1970 Britain's system of money was not based on the decimal system, as is seen in Table 3.1. The £1 unit was made up of 20 shilling units. Each shilling unit was made up of 12 penny units. When the currency was decimalised the rate set was 1 new penny = 2.4 old pennies because 100 new pennies would make up a pound whilst 240 old pennies had previously made up a pound.

Employment: welfare and protection

Once the issue of old age pensions had at last been tackled, Lloyd George was determined to move on to the problem of the hardship caused by loss of earnings due to unemployment and sickness. By the middle of 1908 this was a serious issue because the general economic situation was becoming difficult for the lower income groups. Unemployment was rising and wages were either stationary or falling. At the same time, inflation was reducing the real value of wages by pushing up the cost of living.

At the Board of Trade, Churchill introduced an Act setting up **labour exchanges** in 1909. The aim of this was to make it easier for the unemployed to get in touch with potential employers.

Meanwhile, in 1908, Lloyd George went to Germany to study the German system of **social insurance** at first hand. (A welfare system had been in existence in Germany since the 1880s.) By the autumn of 1908 a team of civil servants were working on the principles of a scheme to introduce unemployment and sickness insurance into Britain.

Key question
What success did the government have in introducing reforms to help the unemployed?

Labour exchanges
Government offices where the unemployed could be helped to find work.

Social insurance
The provision of support to those unable to look after themselves.

Cartoon on old age
pensions.
What point is the
cartoonist making
about the introduction
of old age pensions?

THE NEW YEAR'S GIFT.

**Friendly societies
and Industrial
insurance
companies**
Types of insurance
company providing
policies at cheap
rates to enable to
the less well off to
provide for funeral,
sickness expenses or
injuries suffered at
work.

Key question
Why was there
resistance to
government
intervention?

Although work on the schemes was well advanced by 1909,
their eventual implementation was delayed until the National
Insurance Act of 1911. The first payments under the new laws
were not made until the summer of 1912 (for unemployment)
and the beginning of 1913 (for health).

The delay was mainly because Lloyd George and Churchill,
who were the politicians in charge of the details, wanted to deal
with both sickness and unemployment at the same time.
Unemployment insurance was relatively uncontroversial and, on
its own, could probably have been introduced without any
difficulty in 1909. Sickness benefits, however, were an entirely
different matter.

Opposition to sickness benefits

The reason why there was controversy when it came to sickness
benefits was because there were some powerful vested interests
already operating in this field. The **friendly societies**,
industrial insurance companies and doctors would all be

affected by the intervention of the government into this kind of benefit provision.

The insurance companies and friendly societies collected millions of pounds every year in payments from lower middle-class and better off working-class families. This was to pay for policies covering them for different benefits such as sick pay or doctors' visits. The poorest working-class families could not afford these policies and generally had no protection at all other than charity organisations. It took months of difficult negotiations for Lloyd George to work out and agree suitable safeguards and compromises with the various companies, who were often as suspicious of each other as they were of the government. However, it is worth pointing that many of these societies were working-class organisations which had had served their clients well. Indeed, recent research suggests that they often operated more efficiently and cheaply than the state schemes that replaced them.

There was also opposition from the doctors' organisation, the British Medical Association. This opposition was mainly a result of the influence of the wealthier doctors who feared that the status of their profession would be lowered if they were paid by government. However, the adoption of a 'panel' system, which allowed insured patients to choose their own doctor from a panel of doctors under the control of a local health committee, proved very popular with the less well-off doctors, especially those in the inner cities. They realised that their incomes would rise considerably from this new source of patients.

The National Insurance Act 1911

The National Insurance Act was in two separate parts. Part I dealt with Health Insurance and was the responsibility of the Treasury. Part II dealt with Unemployment Insurance and was the responsibility of the Board of Trade.

Key question
Who was to benefit from National Insurance?

Health insurance provision

The Health Insurance system worked as follows:

- All workers earning less than £160 per year and aged between 16 and 60 were included – around 15 million in all.
- Weekly contributions were taken from the worker (4d), the employer (3d) and the government (2d). This encouraged Lloyd George to coin the slogan '9d, for 4d,' in his attempts to make the idea popular.

The resulting entitlement was:

- Sickness benefit of 10s (50p) per week for 13 weeks (7s 6d for women); 5s (25p) per week for a further 13 weeks after that. Later, the reduced benefit for the second 13-week period was abolished in favour of full benefit for 26 weeks.
- A 30s maternity grant.
- 5s a week disability benefit.
- Free medical treatment under a panel doctor.

Non-working wives and children were not covered by the scheme, nor was hospital treatment – except for admission to a **sanatorium**, which was mainly intended to benefit tuberculosis sufferers.

Key term

Sanatorium
A kind of hospital especially for recovery from long-term debilitating conditions. Emphasis was placed on rest, cleanliness and good ventilation.

THE DOCTOR.
(*With Apologies to Sir Luke Fildes, R.A.*)

PATIENT (*General Practitioner*). "THIS TREATMENT WILL BE THE DEATH OF ME.'
DOCTOR BILL. "I DARE SAY YOU KNOW BEST. STILL THERE'S ALWAYS A CHANCE."

Cartoon depicting Asquith as a doctor. What does the cartoon reveal about the issue of sickness benefit provision?

Unemployment Insurance

The Unemployment Insurance scheme was much less ambitious and covered far fewer workers. In all a total of 2.25 million were protected, mainly in construction and engineering trades, which were susceptible to fluctuating employment levels. The idea was to support workers over a short period of time out of work. It was not meant to tackle the problem of long-term unemployment.

The Unemployment Insurance scheme was as follows:

- Weekly contributions were 2½d each from workers, employers and the government.
- The insured workers were entitled to a payment of 7s per week benefit for up to a maximum of 15 weeks.

Other Liberal achievements in social reform

Numerous other reforms were also undertaken by the Liberal
Governments and can be summarised as follows:

Key question
How widely did the
Liberals' social
reforms range?

- A Trades Disputes Act in 1906 protected trade unions on strike
  from being sued by employers.
- A Workmen's Compensation Act in 1906 brought all categories
  of worker under the provisions for compensation for accidents
  at work and extended protection to cover injury to health.
- A Merchant Shipping Act in 1906 brought in by Lloyd George
  provided tight controls on standards of food and
  accommodation on British Merchant Ships.
- A Coal Mines Act in 1908 introduced a maximum eight-hour
  day for miners.
- A Trade Boards Act in 1909 set up boards to impose minimum
  wages in the so-called 'sweated trades' where low pay and long
  hours had long prevailed. Tailoring, box making, chain making
  and lace making were initially covered. The act was widened to
  include more trades in 1913.
- A Shops Act in 1910 entitled shop assistants to one half-day off
  each week.
- A further Mines Act in 1911 laid down regulations for training,
  safety measures and accident procedures.

Summary diagram: The main Liberal reforms

Date	Act	Description
1906	Education (Provision of Meals) Act	Enabled LEAs to provide school meals for 'needy' children
1907	Education Act	Made school medical inspections for children compulsory
1908	Children's Act	Juvenile courts and remand homes set up
1909	Old Age Pension Act	Pensions to be paid to those aged over 70 who had annual incomes of £21 or less
1909	Budget	Child allowances
1909	Labour exchanges	Set up to make it easier for unemployed to get in touch with employers
1911	National Insurance Act	Unemployment and sickness insurance

3 | Assessing the Liberal Achievement

Key question
How radical were the
social reforms that
were introduced by
the Liberals?

The effect of these social reforms meant a significant increase in
government intervention. The state had now assumed an
unprecedented degree of responsibility for individuals in the
lower classes of society. A great expansion in the civil service was
required to oversee its administration. The sums spent on the
new benefits exceeded all the official estimates.

This welfare legislation entirely by-passed the operations of the
Poor Law and, to a considerable degree, appeared to make the
question of its reform irrelevant. The Unionist Government had
set up a Royal Commission to examine the Poor Laws in 1905.

Key terms

Left-wing historians
Historians tending to reach their conditions based on their political preference for Marxist-Socialist policies.

Capitalist system
Economic system based on private ownership of land and resources and driven by the need to make profits.

Socialism
A social and economic system in which private property in all forms is abolished and the means of production and distribution of wealth are owned by the community as a whole.

By the time it reported in 1909 there was little political interest in any party in a major overhauling of the system. As a result the Poor Law largely fell into disuse until it was finally abolished in 1929.

The overall impact of the Liberals' social reforms has often been criticised as 'too little, too late'. **Left-wing historians** tend to dismiss them as limited concessions aimed at propping up the **capitalist system**.

The reality for people at the time was that by 1912, when the National Insurance provisions began to take effect, a very considerable boost had been given to the incomes of the poorest families. The combined effect of child welfare support, old age pensions, employment legislation, child allowances and National Insurance meant that a significant safety net had been established against poverty. Few poor families could fail to benefit from at least some aspect of this legislation. In particular, the relief to working-class budgets in respect to the support of elderly relatives, brought about by the Old Age Pensions Act, should not be underestimated.

It is not clear how the Liberals could have done much more at the time, given the contemporary views on the limits of taxation, and the fact that their philosophy was 'liberalism' (not 'socialism'), which still recognised a role for individual enterprise and personal responsibility.

Study Guide: AS Questions

In the style of AQA

Read from the following sources and then answer the questions that follow on page 58.

Source A

Adapted from: the Act to provide for old age pensions, 1908.

The conditions for the receipt of an old age pension by any person are:

(1) The person must have attained the age of seventy.

(2) The person must satisfy the pension authorities that for at least twenty years up to the date for the receipt of any pension he has been a British subject, and has had his residence in the United Kingdom.

(3) The person must satisfy the pension authorities that his yearly means do not exceed thirty-one pounds ten shillings [£31.50].

A person shall be disqualified for receiving or continuing to receive an old age pension under this Act if he has regularly failed to work according to his ability, opportunity, and need, for the maintenance or benefit of himself and those legally dependent on him.

Source B

Adapted from: the National Insurance Act, 1911.

The sum required for the payment of unemployment benefit under this Act shall be derived partly from contributions by workmen in the insured trades and partly from contributions by employers of such workmen and partly from money provided by Parliament.

Source C

Adapted from: Michael E. Rose, The Relief of Poverty 1834–1914, *1972.*

It is of course difficult to access the value of the Liberal reforms in terms of their effect on poverty before the outbreak of the First World War. The Old Age Pension Act, confined as it was to the very poor, drastically reduced the numbers of old people who received poor relief. It did little, however, to reduce the numbers in workhouses. The National Insurance Act of 1911 was not brought into operation until 1913, and therefore could have had little impact on poverty before 1914. Unemployment insurance was in any case confined at first to a few skilled trades.

(a) Use Source B and your own knowledge
    Explain briefly what was meant by the term 'the insured trades' in the context of the National Insurance Act.
    (3 marks)

(b) Use Source A and your own knowledge
    Explain how useful Source A is as evidence that the provision of new pensions was restricted. (7 marks)

(c) Use Sources A, B and C and your own knowledge
    'The Old Age Pensions and National Insurance Acts, together with the other welfare reforms of the Liberal governments, had only limited success in dealing with the causes of poverty between 1905 and 1914.'
    Explain why you agree or disagree with this statement.
    (15 marks)

Source: AQA, January 2002

> **Exam tips**
> Look back to the advice on pages 39–40 for this type of AQA question. Try using the same techniques to attempt the questions above.

In the style of Edexcel

(a) Why did the Liberal governments embark on an extensive programme of social reform in the years 1906–11? (15 marks)

Source: Edexcel, January 2002

(b) Describe the achievements of the Liberal Governments in helping the vulnerable sections of society in the period 1906 to 1911.
    (15 marks)

Exam tips

The cross-references are intended to take you straight to the material that will help you to answer the questions.

(a) The 'why' element needs to be the main focus of your answer. This means you have to focus on what the problems being addressed were and use your knowledge of the actual reforms selectively to illustrate your point. For example, it is no use simply telling the examiner about the children's welfare reforms in terms of what they did. You must explain the need for reform along the lines of:

'An act to permit local education authorities to provide school meals paid for out of rates was introduced in order to address the problem of undernourished children in schools. There was strong evidence by 1906 that hungry children could not study properly and as elementary education was by now compulsory and paid for by the taxpayer, the government was under pressure to allow school meals for the most needy children' (page 47).

In this way you are focusing more on 'why' legislation was produced rather than what it entailed. Keep to this formula in discussing the range of legislation.

Credit is also given for any linking of factors – you could show how a range of reasons came together to produce a range reforms that benefited children in different ways. You should also comment on the relative importance of the factors that you refer to even though the wording of the question does not explicitly require this. For example:

- 'The most important reason why old age pensions were introduced was because of the widespread feeling that it was intolerable that the elderly in Britain should be reduced to charity or the Poor Law, when countries such as Germany had had pensions for over twenty years' (page 31).

- 'Overall the main reason why social reform under the Liberals was so extensive was because of the relative neglect of reform by previous governments' (pages 43–4).

This type of comment is needed if your answer is to be put into the highest scoring level.

(b) The main principles for answering this question successfully are as for the causation question above. Here of course you are focusing on describing *what* happened and not *why* it happened. However, in covering the range of social reforms of the period, you need to establish links between the various reforms and to comment on their relative importance. You should also group or categorise achievements.

- For example, you could deal with the Liberal's achievements in introducing measures to improve the health of children: you might show a link between the identification of ill-health of children in schools that the medical inspection legislation was

> intended to address and the subsequent curbs on children buying alcohol and cigarettes (page 48).
>
> - You could comment on which part of the children's legislation had the most immediate beneficial impact (pages 47–8).
>
> You must offer this kind of linking and prioritising of importance to achieve the highest level of marks, even though the question does not formally specify that this is necessary. It is in this way that you are exploring the significance of the Liberal's achievements.

In the style of OCR

1. Study the four sources on poverty and national efficiency, and then answer all the sub-questions.

(a) Study Sources B and C
How far do these two sources differ in their attitudes towards government responsibility for welfare?   (20 marks)

(b) Study all the sources
Using all the sources and your own knowledge, examine the view that, in the period 1900–14, there was growing support for the need for state intervention in the problem of poverty and national efficiency.   (40 marks)

Source: OCR, May 2002

Source A

From: Seebohm Rowntree, Poverty: A Study of Town Life, *1901. A factory owner and researcher of working class life, who concluded that more than a quarter of the population of York were living in poverty, here explains its consequences.*

Let us clearly understand what 'bare physical efficiency' means. A family living on the poverty line must never go into the country unless they walk. The father cannot smoke tobacco and can drink no beer. The mother can never buy any pretty clothes for herself. The children can have no pocket money for toys or sweets. If any of these rules is broken, the extra expenditure can only be met by limiting the diet and sacrificing physical efficiency.

Source B

From: Minority Report of the Royal Commission on the Poor Law and Relief of Distress, 1909. A report by a minority of the members of the Royal Commission suggests that the existing Poor Law should be replaced by a completely new welfare system.

The nation faces today, as it did in 1834, an ever-growing expenditure from public and private funds, resulting in a minimum of prevention and cure, the far-reaching demoralization of character and the continuance of much unrelieved poverty. With regard to the relief of poverty, the Poor Law should now be included in a consistent welfare system. This should be based on recovering the cost from all who are able to pay, exempting those who cannot do so.

Source C

From: Norman Pearson, The Idle Poor, *1911. A middle-class writer argues for a policy to control the idle poor.*

It is to be feared that the habitual vagrant is seldom capable of being reformed. As a rule, he is not an ordinary person, but one who is a pauper in his blood and bones. Broadly speaking, paupers belong to inferior stock, and the community needs to be protected against them. Therefore, the proper authorities should be given the power of segregating and detaining those who burden the present, and endanger the future, of our race.

Source D

From: R.C.K. Ensor, The Practical Case for a Legal Minimum Wage, *1912. A member of the Fabian Society puts the 'national efficiency' case for a minimum wage.*

If the labour unrest of these days indicates a disease in society, then the policy of the legally enforced minimum wage should appeal to moderate and far-seeing statesmen. We all know the findings of Mr Seebohn Rowntree. His figures probably understate the case today because the last decade has seen a steep rise in the cost of living. With low wages, physical efficiency is not maintained. The State should interfere in the matter of wages, just as it has with other problems which destroyed the nation's human resources.

Exam tips

(a) The key here is to stick to the sources and the focus of the question. You are not asked why they differ but it could be useful to point out the origin of the sources, especially if you are aware that the minority report of 1909 represented the views of the more radical reformers on the Royal Commission whose ideas had not found much expression in the official report. 'How far' means that you must present a balanced view, identifying differences but recognising any points of convergence or any ways in which you are not comparing like with like. Clearly B takes a far more sympathetic attitude towards the problem of poverty than that expressed in C. However, it is only fair to C to point out that he is referring to a particular type of person who is habitually idle, not the 'ordinary person' who might fall on hard times through no fault of his own. Pearson is referring to the kind of 'pauper by choice' that the Poor Law was always intended to deter. The minority report is aimed at the more general issue of poverty. It is worth noting that both sources refer to the issue of costs and the social impact of poverty.

(b) There is a need to balance your answer between what can be gleaned from the sources and your own knowledge. Where possible try to elaborate what the sources tell you from your own knowledge where you can. Look for ways to comment on what the origin of the sources adds to the overall picture. For example, Source B, while arguing for a 'consistent welfare system' nevertheless represents a minority view of the Royal Commission. The content of C and D indicates division. However, the question refers to 'growing' support and, taken together, the sources do suggest increasing awareness at least of the problem – A and D, for example, can be linked to suggest this. In dealing with the sources make sure that you group them according to what they say to construct a thematic answer, and refer to each of them at some point in the answer; however, the actual balance of coverage will necessarily depend on the individual content that each source offers. Be clear where you are using your own knowledge to add to the detail obtainable from the sources.

2. To what extent did the social policies of the Liberals 1906–14 address the needs of the working classes?

Exam tips

The cross-references are intended to take you straight to the material that will help you to answer the question.

You need to assess the impact of the social policies as well as identifying what they were.

- For example, when looking at old age pensions, put the actual terms of the Act into context – the age at which pensions became payable against general life expectancy at that time (pages 49–52).
- Take a balanced view – don't write off reforms simply because they don't measure up to modern standards.
- Obviously it is advisable to look for a reasonable range of coverage of different reforms, but don't fall into the trap of overloading the answer with every conceivable reform that you can remember. If you do this it will prove difficult to develop any of them in sufficient depth to score highly. So be selective, choose a fair range of the more important reforms balanced to reflect the needs of different groups:

  – OAPs (pages 49–52)
  – children (pages 47–9)
  – the unemployed (pages 52–3 and 55)
  – the infirm or injured (pages 52–4).

Then make sure that you give a reasonably detailed analysis of these. Remember that the wording of this particular question requires some explanation of what the 'needs of the working classes' were in order to maintain a relevant focus.

In the style of WJEC

(a) Explain briefly the way in which the Liberal Government tried to improve the lives of children from working class families, 1906–8.

(b) To what extent did the Liberal Government's legislation 1906–11 reflect changing attitudes to social reform?

Exam tips

The cross-references are intended to take you straight to the material that will help you to answer the questions.

In WJEC papers the marks are awarded separately for content (one-third) and for approach (two-thirds) to arrive at the total mark. You therefore need to pay particular attention to the supportive detail that you include in your answer.

(a) The emphasis here is on a descriptive explanation, with the marks awarded one-third for content and two-thirds for focus. Make sure you cover a full range of the detail possible as these questions will tend to be focused so as to target a reasonably limited area. Make sure you show how the legislation you identify actually helped the target group. For example:

'Many working class children suffered from inadequate diets which made it difficult for them to work effectively at school. To improve their prospects of learning the Liberals introduced the School Meals Act that allowed local LEAs to provide meals for deprived children and pay for them out of the rates' (page 47).

(b) Give an evaluative answer, but shorter than the full essay style, as it is part of a structured question. Again the marks are awarded one-third for content and two-thirds for approach, so make sure there is an appropriate balance. This question essentially needs the impact of New Liberal thinking to be assessed, while exploring the idea of change and continuity. You would be expected to show how collectivist ideas were expressed in the legislation, e.g. in the National Insurance Act of 1911, while leaving some aspects of *laissez-faire* individualism intact (pages 52–5).

4 The Liberals and Constitutional Reform 1906–14

POINTS TO CONSIDER

By the end of the twentieth century the powers of the House of Lords had become so limited that it was easy to forget how extensive they had been at the century's outset. In the eighteenth and nineteenth centuries the Lords had been seen as more important in many ways than the House of Commons. Its members had higher social status and as hereditary members were not subject to the uncertainty and expense of periodic elections. Prime Ministers were more frequently peers than MPs. Their Cabinet colleagues, especially the more senior ones, were also most likely to be peers.

This period saw the fundamental shift of power taking place away from hereditary political power towards elective political power, which this chapter will examine through the following themes:

- The nature of the dispute with the House of Lords
- The Budget of 1909 and the constitutional crisis it provoked
- The reform of the House of Lords 1911
- The issue of women's right to vote.

Key dates

1903	Women's Social and Political Union formed
1906	Plural Voting Bill to end entitlement to vote in more than one constituency is defeated in the House of Lords
1907	Government passes resolutions in the Commons calling for reform of the House of Lords
1909	House of Lords rejects the Budget
1910	Parliament Bill introduced but rejected by House of Lords
1911	Parliament Act limiting the legislative powers of the House of Lords passed
1912	Government attempt to find a compromise on the issue of votes for women fails
1913	Plural Voting Act finally passed
	'Cat and Mouse' Act

Key question
Why was the political role of the House of Lords controversial?

1 | The Problem of the House of Lords

The House of Lords at the beginning of the twentieth century still had a full range of political powers directly comparable to those of the House of Commons. The only exception in practice was that, by custom, the Lords did not interfere with what were termed 'money bills'; that is, any legislation directly to do with the raising of taxes or the spending of public money. Therefore, the government's annual Finance Bills (or budgets) were passed by the House of Lords without amendment or even debate. In all other cases the Lords could amend or reject any bill any number of times.

By 1900 the majority of adult males had the right to vote and it was clear that, before long, all males would have it. There was even the prospect that women would in the foreseeable future gain the **franchise**. As the electoral system for the House of Commons grew increasingly democratic, so the position of the House of Lords as an unelected chamber in which the right to membership rested on inheritance or direct appointment seemed more obviously unfair. Why should a few hundred privileged individuals be able to overturn the decisions of a House of Commons elected by around eight million voters?

Key terms

Franchise
The terms on which individuals hold the right to vote.

Veto
The right to reject a bill completely.

Nineteenth-century confrontations

During the nineteenth century there were several confrontations between the government and the House of Lords.

The most famous was in 1832 when the government had introduced a bill reforming the electoral system and giving more men the vote. The House of Lords had rejected this bill and it had only been passed when the government threatened to create enough new Lords from their own supporters to ensure that it would pass. The Lords had backed down in 1832, and the precedent had been set that in future conflicts the threat of a mass creation of new peers could be used to ensure that the will of the House of Commons would ultimately prevail over that of the Lords.

In the 1870s, the Conservative Prime Minister, Disraeli, had set out his view on how the House of Lords should conduct itself in the event of future conflicts. Disraeli argued that the Lords should only use its power to **veto** or amend bills with which it disagree where:

- Opinion in the Commons was very divided and the bill had passed by a very narrow majority.
- There was a clear feeling of public opinion against what was being proposed.
- The issue was so fundamental that it could be argued that no government could make such a big change without putting the issue to voters in a general election.

Since Disraeli's time the majority of governments had been Conservative and only one major clash had occurred. This had been in 1893 when Gladstone's last government managed to pass a bill for Irish Home Rule through the Commons (see page 110). The Lords had rejected this bill, arguing that it did not have popular support in the country and depended on the Irish MPs for its majority. This position seemed to fulfil Disraeli's conditions and the Gladstone government did back down on the issue.

However, from 1906 the Liberals had such a massive majority that it was most unlikely that any bills would now be passed by small margins. Also the Liberals were pledged to issues such as social reform and Irish Home Rule during the election campaign. It was therefore unlikely that the House of Lords would be able to use the 'Disraeli Doctrine' to justify interfering with the Liberal Government's bills.

2 | The Constitutional Crisis 1909–11

The origins of the **constitutional crisis**, which was triggered by Lloyd George's budget proposals of 1909 (see pages 68–70), did not lie in House of Lords' opposition to the principles of 'New Liberalism', for example, to the government's welfare reforms. On the contrary, the Unionist leadership generally welcomed the introduction of old age pensions and the reforms affecting children. They even promised to improve upon them if returned to office.

The real roots of the crisis lay in the political helplessness to which the Unionists were reduced in the House of Commons after the 1906 general election. With only 157 MPs the Unionists were almost irrelevant in the Lower House and it was not surprising that they began to consider how they might use their continued predominance in the House of Lords to try to redress the imbalance.

The Unionist leader Balfour had made a rather unwise comment in the heat of the 1906 election campaign, saying that 'the great Unionist Party should still control, whether in power or opposition, the destinies of this great Empire'. This was not intended as a commitment to blanket opposition to a future Liberal Government. In fact it was aimed at the specific issue of Irish Home Rule. Balfour was only too aware that the power of the Lords needed to be used selectively and with caution if it was to be effective. Between 1906 and 1909, therefore, the bills chosen for obstruction by the Unionist peers were identified carefully, in the hope of extracting the maximum embarrassment for the Liberals while steering away from issues where the government might secure popular support.

The 1906 Education Bill
The first confrontation came in 1906 over the government's proposed Education Bill. This amounted to a political pay-off to the Nonconformists for their support following the Education Act of 1902 (see pages 10–14). The Liberal Government felt indebted to its Nonconformist supporters and was committed to addressing their grievances. Therefore, despite the fact that some members of the Cabinet privately accepted the value of the 1902 Act it was

Key question
Why did relations between the Liberal Government and the House of Lords become strained after the 1906 general election?

Constitutional crisis
A political crisis where the issues provoking the crisis relate to the rules under which the country is governed.

Key term

decided to introduce a bill to meet some of the Nonconformists' objections to it.

The 1906 Education Bill proposed that all Church of England schools should be taken over by the local authorities, who would appoint teachers without applying religious tests. Previously teachers had to be Anglican. Only general religious teaching, not specific to any religion, would be allowed. An exception to this was in areas where four-fifths of parents requested a specific type of religious doctrine to be taught, and even then only where there was sufficient choice of school provision unconnected to particular Churches. This exception was designed to help the Roman Catholic Church whose existing schools were already operating over and above the normal local requirement for places.

The provisions of this Education Bill angered the Anglicans as much as the 1902 Act had enraged the Nonconformists. A compromise was sought, with both the Archbishop of Canterbury and the king eventually becoming involved. Balfour had planned that controversial legislation should be opposed initially in the Commons and then amended to reach a compromise in the Lords. In this first test, however, the strategy failed since it proved impossible to hammer out a compromise that both sides could accept. Consequently, the government was forced to withdraw the bill, which they had seen as forming the centrepiece of their programme for the session.

The Lords rejected two other major bills in the period 1906–8:

- a bill to end **plural voting**
- a licensing bill aimed at further restrictions on the sale and consumption of alcohol.

This hardly amounted to a wholesale wrecking of the government's legislative programme. On the contrary, the targets were carefully selected. Significantly, trade union reform in 1906 was allowed to pass even though this allowed trade unions protection from being sued by their employers over strikes. Also, all of the social reforms detailed in Chapter 3 went through. This was because they realised it would be counter-productive to reject reforms with a wide popular appeal.

The government's response 1907–8

The intention of the Unionists was to try to confuse and demoralise the Liberals. They had some success in this. By 1907 the government was trying to decide whether or not to confront the peers. One major problem was the lack of a really popular cause with which to appeal to the electorate. The Education Bill was important to certain sections of the Liberal Party, but it was not a matter of great importance to the public at large.

In 1907, therefore, Campbell-Bannerman did no more than introduce **resolutions** into the Commons calling for limitations on the power of the Lords to delay, amend or veto legislation. These resolutions were passed by a huge majority since they were supported not only by Liberals but also by Labour and the Irish

Key terms

Plural voting
An individual's right to vote in more than one constituency, e.g. if the place of residence and ownership of business premises were in two different areas.

Resolutions
Statements that are voted upon in principle but which, if passed, have no force in law.

Key dates

Plural Voting Bill to end entitlement to vote in more than one constituency was defeated in the House of Lords: 1906

Government passed resolutions in the Commons calling for reform of the House of Lords: 1907

Nationalists. They remained, however, no more than a warning shot at the Upper House. When the 1908 session of Parliament opened, reform of the House of Lords remained conspicuously absent from the government's proposals.

It was not surprising that the government failed to address the issue of the powers of the Lords in 1908, since the Cabinet was entirely undecided over what to do.

- Some, like Campbell-Bannerman, simply wished to curb the power of the peers over legislation.
- However, others, including Sir Edward Grey, preferred to make reform of the composition of the Lords the priority.

Some moderate Unionist peers themselves were in favour of the latter course and there had even been a proposal from them to end automatic hereditary entry to the Lords during 1907. This proposition had been opposed by both the government and the more right-wing Unionist peers, though for differing reasons. The right-wing peers opposed any interference with the Lords' powers or composition. The government feared that reform of the composition of the Lords would make it harder, in the end, to justify limiting their legislative powers.

The political climate in 1907 and 1908 was hardly encouraging for the Liberals. Overall, the trend in by-election results was against them and most commentators expected a considerable Unionist revival when the next general election came.

Despite the introduction of old age pensions and child welfare reform, there was little improvement in the political fortunes of the Liberals by the beginning of 1909. The problem was that, however deserving these two groups might be of the government's attention, neither actually amounted to much in electoral terms. The government therefore urgently needed something compelling with which to regain the political initiative.

Fortunately for them there was soon a very obvious issue upon which to make a stand.

The Budget of 1909

The Budget for 1909 was going to have to be a major reforming piece of legislation. There was no alternative to this because increasing expenditure on defence, along with increased spending on social welfare, meant that taxation had to be increased. Politically, the government could not risk cutting back in either sector but nor could it fund both from its existing revenue. As Lloyd George became increasingly aware of the extent of the future **budget deficits**, so he and Asquith exerted increasing pressure on the rest of the Cabinet to agree to an extensive reform of taxation.

It was an accepted constitutional practice that the House of Lords could not amend or reject financial legislation. However, as rumours grew that the 1909 budget would contain radical proposals, speculation mounted that the Lords might consider breaking with tradition on the grounds that the budget went beyond normal financial provisions. In the event, some of

Key question
Why was the Budget of 1909 so significant?

Budget deficit
Occurs when more is being spent than raised in taxes – a gap that can only be filled by borrowing.

Key term

Cartoon depicting Lloyd George as a giant threatening the rich. How reliable is this cartoon for an understanding of the 1909 budget? A 'plutocrat' is a person with great wealth.

RICH FARE.

THE GIANT LLOYD-GORGIBUSTER: "FEE, FI, FO, FAT,
I SMELL THE BLOOD OF A PLUTOCRAT;
BE HE ALIVE OR BE HE DEAD,
I'LL GRIND HIS BONES TO MAKE MY BREAD."

Asquith and Lloyd George's colleagues objected to the proposals. This produced a row within the Cabinet, which became public, over naval spending, which Lloyd George wanted to limit as far as possible.

It was hardly the best background against which to launch a revival of the government's fortunes and there is little doubt that, far from being aimed at provoking confrontation, the Budget was intended to strike enough of a balance to pass without causing a crisis with the Lords. This, however, was a forlorn hope.

In the 1909 Budget Lloyd George proposed to:

- Raise income tax on incomes over £3000 per annum to 1s 2d (6p) from the standard rate of 9d (4p) and bring in an additional tax of 6d (2½p) in the pound on incomes over £5000 per annum.
- Increase duties on spirits, tobacco, liquor licences and **stamp duties**.

Key term

Stamp duty
A tax paid to the government for legalising official or legal documents, e.g. on the sale of property.

- Increase **death duties** on estates valued between £5000 and £1 million pounds.
- Introduce land taxes on:
  - the increased value of land when it changed hands (20 per cent)
  - the annual value of land (1½d in £)
  - the annual value of land leased to mining companies (1s in £).
- Set up a road fund for building and maintaining roads by putting taxes on petrol and introducing licences for motor vehicles.
- Introduce child allowances at a rate of £10 a year for every child under the age of 16. This was payable to families with an annual income of less than £500.

Opposition to the Budget

Concern about the Budget and even opposition to it became more widespread:

- Many Liberals (including some in the Cabinet) had their doubts.
- The Irish Nationalist MPs opposed the duty on spirits fearing it would damage the whiskey export trade, which was vital to employment, especially in Dublin.
- The brewers and distillers were obviously outraged as they would have to pay duty.
- The motorists (not so large a lobby then, of course, as they would later become) were similarly unimpressed.
- Most of all, landowners felt that they were being subjected to unfair treatment and they were particularly incensed by Lloyd George's plan to set up a Development Commission, one of whose tasks would be to carry out a comprehensive land valuation survey to provide the basis for calculating the new taxation on land. This seemed to be the thin end of a socialist wedge, which in future years could be used to attack wealth and force a redistribution of property on a significant scale.

Initially Balfour and Lord Lansdowne (the Unionist leader in the House of Lords) did not intend that the Lords should go so far as to reject the Budget. They instead wanted to extract compromises that would undermine the Budget and keep up the mounting pressure on the government. This, however, was a miscalculation. Neither Balfour nor Lansdowne appreciated at first the limited room for manoeuvre that each side had.

Lansdowne, in particular, underestimated the emotions that had been raised among the rank-and-file Unionist peers. A major reason for this was the fact that the Unionist leaders did not view the Budget in quite the same way as their supporters. To the latter the Budget proposals were an outright attack on the rights of property; the former were much more concerned about the future political implications that the proposals raised for Unionist policies.

Key term

Death duty
Taxes levied on the property or money left by a person when they die.

Key question
Why did the 1909 Budget lead to a constitutional crisis?

The issue of tariff reform

The crux of the problem was that, by 1909, Unionism had effectively been won over to tariff reform (see pages 21–2). One of the key arguments of the tariff reformers was that large-scale social reform could only be funded effectively through the money that would be raised through taxing imports. The Liberals' Budget, by proposing a method of funding social reform while preserving free trade, therefore cut right to the heart of any popular appeal that tariff reform might have. The government knew this only too well and saw that this was a golden opportunity to underpin free trade once and for all and make the Unionists seem even more irrelevant.

Thus the budget crisis of 1909 was in essence an extension of the free trade versus protectionism debate (see page 14) and both sides believed that their political fortunes were at stake in its outcome.

It was the Unionists who were in the more difficult position. It was not easy to turn their case into a popular campaign since it involved some fairly complex arguments about the relationship between tariff reform, taxation, and spending on both social welfare and defence. The government had the much easier task of presenting the issue as simply one of the selfishness of a privileged class. By-elections in the summer of 1909 showed a swing to the Liberals and underlined the fact that the government was winning the argument in the country.

General election January 1910

Balfour and Lansdowne were increasingly driven into a corner. Surrender would split the party because of the expectations of resistance that had been raised, while resistance could only lead to a constitutional crisis. In the event, the matter was taken out of their hands since Lansdowne effectively lost control of the Unionist peers who decided to act as they saw fit. In November 1909 the Lords rejected the Budget and Asquith immediately asked for the dissolution of Parliament and a general election.

The general election of January 1910 produced results that were unsatisfactory for almost everybody (see Table 4.1).

Key date

House of Lords rejected the Budget: 1909

Table 4.1: General election results 1910

Party	No. of seats
Liberals	275
Unionists	273
Labour	40
Irish Nationalists	82

The Liberals could continue in office but only as a minority government. Their immediate problem with the Budget was solved because there was still a majority for it in the Commons. The Irish were prepared to support it in spite of their concerns about whiskey duty. Their support, however, came at a price. They wanted Home Rule for Ireland. However, since a Home

Rule Bill stood no chance of passing an unreformed House of Lords, they wanted a Parliament Bill to limit the Lords' powers to be passed first. In the circumstances the Liberal Government had little option but to agree to this. Ordinary Liberal MPs were demanding as much anyway.

In view of the result of the election the Lords had no choice but to pass the Budget, but the battle had now moved on to the question of their powers and most peers were set on a confrontation.

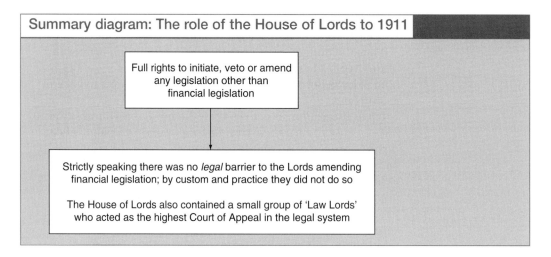

Summary diagram: The role of the House of Lords to 1911

Full rights to initiate, veto or amend any legislation other than financial legislation

Strictly speaking there was no *legal* barrier to the Lords amending financial legislation; by custom and practice they did not do so

The House of Lords also contained a small group of 'Law Lords' who acted as the highest Court of Appeal in the legal system

3 | The Reform of the House of Lords 1911

The Parliament Bill

The Parliament Bill that the government introduced in 1910 contained no surprises. It stated that:

- The Lords could not reject or amend financial legislation.
- There would be a limit of two rejections or amendments on other legislation in successive sessions within the life of a Parliament.
- The maximum duration of a Parliament (i.e. the length of time between general elections) was reduced from seven to five years. This was actually a concession to the Lords since it reduced the time a government with a majority had to pass laws before facing a new election.

In practice this meant that the Lords could expect to delay legislation for a minimum period of two years, assuming that the proposals were immediately passed again by the Commons after each rejection. The Lords resisted this to the bitter end but to no avail. The death of King Edward VII in May 1910 gave them a temporary respite since Asquith was anxious not to appear to be pressing the new king, George V, too soon on the question of creating new peers. However, the delay was brief and by the end of 1910 Asquith was ready to call a second election, this time armed with the mandate to create as many new peers as might be necessary to see the Parliament Bill through.

Key question
Should the outcome of the constitutional crisis be seen as a success or a failure for the Liberal Government?

Key dates

Parliament Bill
introduced but
rejected by House of
Lords: 1910

Parliament Act
passed: 1911

The result of the general election of December 1910 produced no real change in the political balance. The Irish and Labour both advanced marginally to 84 and 42 seats respectively; the Liberals and Unionists tied on 272 seats each. This left the government in a position to force through the bill.

In August 1911, after Asquith had publicly threatened a mass creation of peers, the Parliament Bill was finally passed. Even then some of the moderate Unionist peers had to be drafted in to vote for the government in order to ensure that the bill was not voted down by the 'last-ditchers', some of whom by now had so lost their grip on reality that they preferred to bring the Lords to a 'glorious death' rather than relent.

Attempts at compromise

The constitutional crisis was a classic case of political miscalculations that led to political passions running out of control. This was most obviously the case on the Unionist side, but the government had also miscalculated the impact that the Budget would have. Asquith was eventually forced into threatening a mass creation of peers that was very much against his inclination. Lloyd George raised passions to fever pitch during the summer of 1909 with highly provocative speeches designed to whip up support for the Budget and put pressure on the Lords.

However, despite his revolutionary utterances, Lloyd George was not really intent on destroying the wealthy classes. On the contrary, during the same period, he was employing his considerable abilities to the task of becoming wealthy himself through various business interests. During 1910 the political leaders on both sides had tried, behind the scenes, to control and restore some order to the situation.

Between June and November 1910, a series of meetings was held between the Liberal and Unionist leaders aimed at finding a compromise. This process, known as the 'Constitutional Conference', failed in the end to find a solution but it was a sign that both sides had realised that things were getting out of hand.

In August, Lloyd George proposed a coalition government be set up, with an agenda covering all the major issues of the day – economic, social and constitutional – so as to seek compromise solutions for them all. Balfour was much attracted to this idea in theory, but doubted whether it was practical given the political climate. Asquith was also interested, but both leaders found a hostile response within their parties and the scheme came to nothing.

The results of the constitutional crisis

The outcome of the constitutional crisis was scarcely revolutionary.

- Its most immediate effect was to make the Liberal Government more dependent on the Irish Nationalists.
- It did not result in a flood of legislation needing to be forced through the Lords since the government's reforms since 1906 had already been extensive.

- Its chief victim was Balfour, who paid the penalty for a failed campaign that he had never wanted in the first place. Late in 1911, faced with mounting criticism of his leadership, he decided upon a dignified stepping down rather than await the inevitable and distasteful *coup*. He was succeeded by the relatively unknown Andrew Bonar Law, who had entered Parliament only in 1900, and whose chief qualification was that he was a compromise candidate at a time when other leading contenders, if chosen, might have split the party.
- The crisis cost the Liberals their overall majority and exposed them to the demands of the Irish Nationalists. The reputations of their leaders, particularly Asquith and Lloyd George, were enhanced, but the necessity of dealing with Irish Home Rule meant that the government was bound to face a new constitutional crisis almost immediately.
- It should be remembered, however, that Home Rule was not a new policy for the Liberals. It had not been forced on them by the Irish Nationalists – it had been an official party commitment for over 20 years.

4 | The Women's Suffrage Campaign

One constitutional issue that the Liberals failed to resolve was the difficult matter of the claim of women to be able to vote in parliamentary elections. On the surface it appeared to be a fairly straightforward matter of basic logic and individual rights.

The nineteenth century

During the second half of the nineteenth century women had made steady, if unspectacular, progress in legal and educational emancipation. The employment of women in clerical posts had expanded enormously and they had even made some inroads in the professions. An obvious target for similar progress was political rights.

The question of granting the parliamentary franchise to women on the same terms as men in borough seats was raised during the passage of the 1867 Reform Act. Although rejected, the inconsistency of a system that granted votes to men, who might in their turn be employed by women, was obvious enough. During the course of the nineteenth century they did, however, gain some political rights:

- In 1869 women gained the vote in town council elections in the **municipal boroughs**.
- In 1870 they gained the right to be elected to the School Boards set up under the Education Act.
- From 1875 women could be elected to serve as Poor Law Guardians running the local workhouses.
- In 1889 they were included in the local government franchise, although they did not have the right to take office on the new County and County Borough Councils.

Suffrage groups

The NSWS

The first properly organised group to campaign nationally for the right of women to vote was the National Society for Women's Suffrage (NSWS) formed in 1868. It was an amalgamation of locally based groups that had developed during the 1860s. This group split up in 1888 because some members wanted to affiliate to the Liberal Party while others wanted to be independent of party politics. However, in 1897 a new body was formed that was able to reunite the old NSWS members and bring in various other women's suffrage groups which had been springing up randomly.

The NUWSS

This new organisation was known as the National Union of Women's Suffrage Societies (NUWSS). By 1900 the NUWSS had some 400 branches all over the country and appeared to be a united and forceful pressure group. However, there was a new divisive issue waiting to bring further discord to their campaign.

There were two different approaches among those who wished to see the political emancipation of women. Some argued for the immediate inclusion of women in the franchise on exactly the same terms as men. Others wished to press for the right of all men and women over the age of 21 to vote. There was a danger in this second option from the women's point of view. This was the fear that it was so radical that it might lead to compromises such as had happened with the gradual enfranchisement of men. If this happened one possible outcome might be that all men might get the vote but no women. Once that position had been established women arguably might find it even more difficult to secure the parliamentary vote.

The WSPU

Key date

Women's Social and Political Union formed: 1903

The difference of opinion led to a split within the ranks of the NUWSS. Emmeline Pankhurst, a widow whose husband had been a long-time Liberal campaigner for women's rights, formed a new movement called the Women's Social and Political Union (WSPU) in 1903. Mrs Pankhurst took the view that women should have immediate equality with men in the existing system of voting qualifications. Once this was achieved, attention could turn to campaigning for full democracy.

Mrs Pankhurst had already broken her political connection with the Liberals, in favour of the Independent Labour Party (ILP) (see Chapter 5) believing it to be a better vehicle for her aims of economic and social equality for women. Now, assisted by her daughters, Christabel and Sylvia, she mobilised the WSPU to press the issue of the female suffrage within the ILP.

The relationship between the WSPU and ILP

The problem for the Pankhursts was that the ILP was itself divided over the issue. Most of the leaders were genuinely in favour of the basic idea of the right of women to vote. However, some ILP leaders, such as Keir Hardie, were sympathetic to the Pankhursts' demand for immediate female suffrage on equal terms with men, while others, such as Philip Snowden, later to be a Labour Chancellor of the Exchequer, preferred to wait for complete adult suffrage.

Whichever view they took, the ILP leaders were also uncomfortably aware of the extent of hostility to female equality among working-class males, particularly within the trade unions, for whom female equality in the workplace was unthinkable. In 1905, Keir Hardie introduced a private member's bill to extend the vote to women on the existing franchise. This was the highpoint of WSPU/ILP collaboration and Mrs Pankhurst worked with Keir Hardie to promote the bill. Its defeat was certain, however, and the lack of real enthusiasm for it within the ILP rank and file members left the Pankhursts disappointed and disillusioned.

The WSPU still helped Labour candidates in the 1906 general election campaign but this only increased their anger as some Labour candidates rejected their help while others made it clear that they expected them to restrict their activities to making tea and passing around refreshments at meetings. Mrs Pankhurst was now convinced that women must seize the initiative themselves and secure their own political destiny.

The Liberals' view on female suffrage

Key question
How did the Liberals react to the issue of 'votes for women'?

When the Liberals came to power in 1905, they were also divided over female suffrage. Some, still following Gladstone's views, were opposed to it altogether while others, although sympathetic, were uncertain how best to proceed. For the Liberals the dilemma was that any kind of piecemeal or gradual enfranchisement of women based on property qualifications seemed most likely to benefit the Unionists. The results of granting full adult suffrage were difficult to assess, especially with the Labour Party's ultimate political appeal still an unknown quantity.

In the 1906 election, many Liberal candidates expressed their support for female suffrage, raising hopes among women campaigners that legislation might soon materialise. This was a false hope. In reality the Liberal Government had no intention, in 1906, of risking a political controversy over female suffrage. The most they would do was to remove the obvious anomaly of the exclusion of women from sitting on local councils, by passing the Qualification of Women Act of 1907. This was naturally welcomed by the WSPU, but it hardly constituted a great leap forward, nor was it an acceptable commitment for the future.

Militancy

Frustrated by the lack of progress, the WSPU became more militant. Harassment of politicians at meetings, already employed during the 1906 campaign, was intensified. From such traditional tactics the WSPU graduated to:

• attacks on property: window smashing, arson

- the destruction of mail: pepper-filled letters were dispatched to politicians to provide a literally irritating reminder to the recipients of the women's displeasure with the lack of progress.

The more aggressive the WSPU became however, the harder any kind of concession became for the government, as it could not be seen to be giving in to violence. The more entrenched the government's position became the more intense the anger of the women became. Criminal proceedings resulted in imprisonments that led to hunger strikes, which in turn led the prison authorities to resort to force-feeding. It was an embarrassing state of affairs for any government, especially one calling itself 'Liberal', but, as with the constitutional crisis itself, neither side had a great deal of room for manoeuvre.

The Conciliation Bill

Following the pattern of the Lord–Commons clash (see pages 68–70), both sides tried to extricate themselves from the mess. After the campaign leading up to the 1910 general election, during which Liberal ministers had come in for some rough treatment at the hands of women activists, the WSPU called for a truce in the hope that the gesture would ease the deadlock.

Parliament, rather than the government, responded with a 'Conciliation' Bill drafted by an all-party committee. It proposed the enfranchisement of women, on the basis of either a householder or an occupation franchise, which would have meant in practice nearly eight per cent of women getting the vote. On its second reading, this proposal had a majority of 110. The WSPU welcomed the bill and had high hopes that it was the long-awaited breakthrough.

However, the bill was doomed to failure because some leading Cabinet ministers opposed it from the start:

- Asquith was against it: he was not a supporter of female suffrage anyway and had been deeply angered by the militancy of the recent campaigns. To him, concessions now smacked of giving in to fanatics.
- Other leading Liberals, like Lloyd George, were against it because they saw it as enfranchising the most conservative-minded sections of women and in the long run damaging to the Liberals' electoral chances.

It is only fair to point out that Sylvia Pankhurst, the most socialist-minded of the Pankhurst family, who now focused mainly on her work among the poor of East London, also doubted the wisdom of the bill for this same reason. Asquith's opposition ended the hopes for a Conciliation Bill in 1910. He made vague promises of a government bill to replace it but would not commit himself to a timetable.

The loss of the Conciliation Bill ended the truce that had been declared by the WSPU. There was a mass demonstration and some violent episodes at the end of 1910, after which the truce was resumed in the hope of a fresh initiative. Asquith's next move, however, was to announce, at the end of 1911, the introduction of a Franchise Bill in the next session of Parliament. This was to be aimed at full adult male suffrage. The WSPU was incensed and, from this point onwards, the bitter confrontation between them and the government continued until the outbreak of the First World War, when the Pankhursts changed tack by adopting a patriotic line, and pressing for the full participation of women in the war effort. In the meantime, the government withdrew the Franchise Bill and opted for the abolition of plural voting instead (see page 67).

Deadlock

The failure to make progress on female suffrage, the deterioration of the campaign into terrorism and the dubious morality of the government's tactics made this a grim and discreditable episode

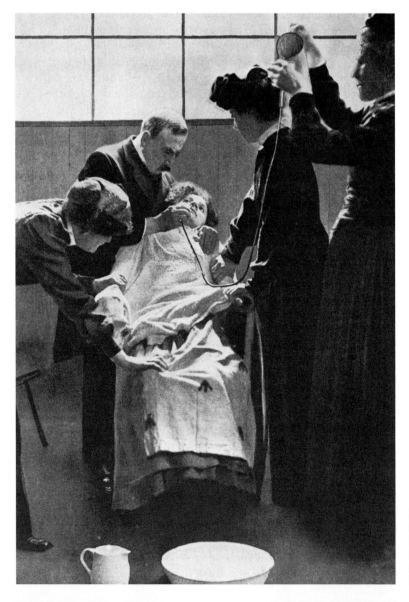

In this propaganda item published in London in 1912, a suffragist on hunger strike is being force fed through the nose.

in political life before the First World War. The government was reduced to 'illiberal' expedients such as the 'Cat and Mouse' Act of 1913, under which women on hunger strike were released and then rearrested, to try to control the situation.

Key date

'Cat and Mouse' Act: 1913

The WSPU leaders became hunted refugees and Christabel Pankhurst fled to Paris to continue her direction of operations. The main blame for the situation, as it existed by 1914, must lie with Asquith, as Prime Minister, because he had passed over the chance to engineer some kind of compromise out of the Conciliation Bill in 1910. A lesser responsibility lies with the leadership of the WSPU for allowing their campaign to get so far out of hand that their actions began to blur the essential justice of their demands.

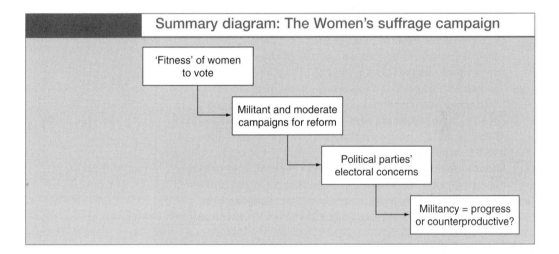

Summary diagram: The Women's suffrage campaign

'Fitness' of women to vote

Militant and moderate campaigns for reform

Political parties' electoral concerns

Militancy = progress or counterproductive?

Study Guide: AS Questions

In the style of AQA

Read the following source and then answer the questions that follow.

Adapted from: Paul Adelman, The Decline of the Liberal Party, 1910–1931, 1981.

As a result of the Lords' rejection of Lloyd George's 'People's Budget', the ending of the House of Lords' veto over the Commons' legislation, which had been used with such obvious one-sidedness during the past three years, became inevitable.

(a) Comment on 'the House of Lords' veto over Commons' legislation' in the context of the years 1906 to early 1909.
(3 marks)

(b) Explain why the House of Lords rejected the 'People's Budget' in November 1909. (7 marks)

(c) How successful were the Liberal governments in achieving welfare reform between 1906 and 1911? (15 marks)

Source: AQA, January 2003

Exam tips

The cross-references are intended to take you straight to the material that will help you to answer the questions.

The source here is a stimulus only. The question is essentially testing your own knowledge.

(a) Explain how the veto worked, i.e. the right to reject completely or amend any legislation sent from the Commons. Then explain how it was used in practice. For full marks show how it was used selectively and give a couple of examples of this (page 65).

(b) Here you need to be explicit about what the Budget contained. You will only receive low marks if your comments are too general, e.g. 'the Budget aimed to increase taxes and the Peers objected to this'. You need to show what new taxes were proposed and why these in particular upset the House of Lords. So, for example, refer to the proposed assessments of land values with taxes to be raised on profits of sales that the Lords saw as direct wealth taxes (page 70).

(c) The key with any evaluative question of this kind is always achieving a balanced answer that recognises the positive aspects of the legislation while drawing appropriate attention to its limitations. Do not go for blanket coverage of the reforms at the expense of more detailed development of the more important reforms. You could start with a brief overview of what problems 'welfare reforms' were meant to address in the context of the period (pages 46–7). Make sure you offer a clearly defined judgement that fits with the balance of the evidence you use in the answer.

In the style of Edexcel

(a) Why, in the years 1910–11, was the Liberal Government able to overcome the resistance of the House of Lords to political and constitutional change? (15 marks)

Source: Edexcel, June 2002

(b) Describe the main features of the Constitutional Crisis 1909–11 and its outcome. (15 marks)

Exam tips

The cross-references are intended to take you straight to the material that will help you to answer the questions.

(a) This is a difficult question because the period specified is very short and therefore implies an in-depth coverage. However, you can use material from outside the period provided that you can show it is relevant. So, for example, 'One reason why the Liberals were able to make a case for reforming the House of Lords was that the Lords had been seen to misuse their power in the period 1906–9 by selectively disrupting the government's legislation on …'. For the rest think widely and don't dismiss anything as too obvious:

- The Liberals had had a massive majority in the period 1906–9 but this had not stopped the Lords using their veto (page 71).
- In using their veto on the Budget in 1909 they had appeared to overstep their constitutional rights (pages 68–71).
- Despite the loss of their overall majority in January 1910 the Liberals could still count on the support of the Irish National Party and the Labour Party, which meant that they still had a comfortable majority over the Conservatives (pages 71–2).
- Although there was 'die-hard' resistance from some peers the official leadership of the Conservatives was more moderate and prepared to compromise in the end (page 73).
- Linked to the previous point, in the end some Conservative peers agreed to stay away from the crucial votes in the House of Lords, while others actually agreed to vote for the government (page 73).
- The government held the trump-card of being able to call upon the king in the last resort to create enough new peers to push the legislation through if the Lords would not back down (pages 72–3).

Make sure that you look to establish links between the various factors and remember to comment on their relative importance.

(b) The formula for this is very similar to the causation question style, except that here you are focused on *what* happened rather than *why* it happened. You still need to comment on linkages between the different stages you describe. A simple example of this might be a comment such as:

'One consequence of the rejection of the Budget by the Lords was to raise again the whole issue of an hereditary chamber overruling the wishes of an elected chamber' (pages 71–2).

You also need to comment on the relative importance of different aspects of the features you are describing. For example:

'The most important outcome of the constitutional crisis was the loss of the government's overall majority. The Liberals had overcome the resistance of the Lords, but at the cost of making themselves dependent on the support of the Irish National Party in the future in a 'hung' parliament' (pages 71–2).

In the style of OCR

1. Study the four sources on militancy and women's suffrage 1906–1914, and then answer all the sub-questions.

   (a) Study Sources A and C
     Compare these sources as evidence for attitudes towards militancy.   (20 marks)
   (b) Study all the sources
     Using all the sources and your own knowledge, assess the view that militancy did more harm than good to the cause of women's suffrage during the period 1906–14.
                                               (40 marks)

Source: OCR, June 2003

Source A

From: Millicent Fawcett, a private letter, November 1910. A leading suffragist, writing to a friend, criticises the militant actions of the WSPU.

I do think these personal assaults of the past five years are extraordinarily silly. The Prime Minister's statement on the possibility of a Bill for women's suffrage was not exactly all we wanted. But it was better than anything offered before. It made The Times say the next day that it put the women's suffrage question definitely before the country at the coming general election, and that if there is a Liberal majority it will be a mandate to the government to grant women the vote. And then these idiots go out smashing windows and bashing ministers' hats over their eyes.

Source B

From: The Clarion, June 1913. A pro-suffragette Labour newspaper comments on the Liberal Government's actions.

The women are winning again. Morale is high. What they lost by window-smashing has been restored to them by the Government's new Cat and Mouse Act rushed through Parliament. Consider what it means. The Spanish Inquisition never invented anything so cruel! 'Wait-and-See Asquith' has tried both force and trickery against them. But the fact is undeniable that the bravery of the women had beaten him.

Source C

From: Emmeline Pankhurst, My Own Story, *1914. A suffragette leader defends the growing militancy of the WSPU.*

In the year 1906 there was an immensely large public opinion in favour of women's suffrage. But what good did that do the cause? We called upon the public for more than sympathy. We called upon it to give women votes. We have tried every means, including processions and meetings, which were not successful. We have tried demonstrations, and now at last we have to break windows. I wish I had broken more. I am not in the least sorry.

Source D

From: Viscount Ullswater, A Speaker's Commentaries, *1925. James Lowther (later Viscount Ullswater) comments on the effects of the suffragette violence on Parliament's attitude to the women's cause. Lowther was the Speaker of the House of Commons during the period of suffragette militancy. He had been a Conservative MP and was personally opposed to women's suffrage.*

By 1913, the activities of the militant suffragettes had reached a stage at which nothing was safe from their attacks. The feeling in the House of Commons, caused by these lawless actions, hardened the opposition to the demands of the suffragettes. As a result, on 6 May the private member's bill* that would have given women the vote, for which the Government had promised parliamentary time so that it could become law, was rejected by the House of Commons by a majority of forty seven.

[*'Private member's bill' = a parliamentary bill started by an ordinary MP, rather than by the government.]

Exam tips

(a) Focus on and refer to the issue of the 'attitudes' shown in the two sources. Avoid being drawn into a general account of the different approaches of suffragists and suffragettes disconnected from the source material. The key issue to focus on is the question of the attitude to militancy in terms of what it might achieve. Clearly, Source A sees this in negative terms and argues that the progress being made, while not as great as might be desired, is still progress and is compromised by the actions of 'idiots'. Source C argues to the contrary, seeing militancy as the only way to achieve the desired outcome. It is valid to consider the origins of the source in the comparison to the extent that they come from different years: Source A is a private letter in response to events in 1910 when there were two general elections and hopes for a breakthrough of sorts were high, whereas Source C was written for publication to justify militancy and comes from 1914 when these hope had still come to nothing.

(b) 'Assess the view' is telling you to come up with a balanced judgement of your own.

- Make sure you use all the sources and the information in them both in their own terms and as the basis of elaborating your own knowledge.
- Group the sources according to what they say and construct a thematic answer.
- Be clear where you are using your own knowledge to add to the detail contained in the sources.
- Make sure you focus your comments on the 'more harm than good' issue and that you have a clear view on this.
- Try to classify the overall position of each: Sources A and D see militancy negatively; B and C see it more positively.
- Try also to sum up the overall balance of the evidence. Use the origin of the sources and your own knowledge in combination, where you can, to shed light on the value of the evidence. For example, it could be argued that Source D is particularly useful because its evidence comes with the benefit of hindsight in 1925 when women have actually gained the vote and the debate has become somewhat academic as a consequence. The other sources are part of the actual campaign period and as such possibly reflect the passions roused by the events rather more than D.

2. **(a)** To what extent was the outcome of the constitutional crisis of 1909–11 a triumph for the Liberals in 1911?

   (b) How successful was Asquith as Prime Minister from 1908 to 1914? (Do not discuss foreign policy in your answer.)

Source: OCR, January 2003

Exam tips

The cross-references are intended to take you straight to the material that will help you to answer the questions.

(a) As always with this type of question the key is to reach a balanced judgement that is best delivered at the start and then supported by the rest of your answer. As a general rule go for development of a few key themes rather than breadth of coverage, although in this particular answer this is easy because the range is limited anyway. Here you are best advised to build your answer around the opposing issues of the limitations eventually imposed on the powers of the Lords against the results of the 1910 elections, which deprived the Liberals of their overall majority and left them dependent on the Irish National Party, who demanded Home Rule as the price of their support.

(b) A standard evaluative question requiring a clear judgement balanced between the conflicting viewpoints and evidence. As always with essays of this kind it is vital not to spread your coverage too thinly, so resist the temptation to bring in every possible aspect of the events; instead, concentrate on a reasonable coverage of the most central issues in more depth. You need to have clear criteria to assess 'successful' in this type of question, for example against aims, results or context. Marks are given for the development of the arguments, so plan your response before you try to answer. Think about what the role of the Prime Minister required – not just the actual policies, but leading the government and especially the Cabinet. The main content areas to look at are:

- The implementation of social reforms: remember that many traditional Liberals were not entirely comfortable with some of the measures (pages 45–6).
- The handling of the budget crisis and the ensuing constitutional crisis: Asquith's support for Lloyd George, the criticisms of his handling of the king and the question of the creation of Liberal peers (pages 66–73).
- Ireland: this is not a foreign policy issue and so must receive consideration (page 114).
- Female suffrage: particularly important because of Asquith's own opposition to the idea (page 76).

5 The Rise of the Labour Party 1895–1918

POINTS TO CONSIDER

During the course of the twentieth century the Labour Party emerged as one of the two great political parties in Britain competing for power with the Conservatives. Its rise was accompanied by the decline of the Liberal Party. This chapter will consider the question of whether the Labour Party from its origins showed signs that it was destined to achieve its later status or whether it simply benefited from events. It will do this through the following themes:

- The origins of the Labour Party
- The Labour Party in the Commons 1906–14
- The trade unions and industrial unrest 1910–14
- The Labour Party and the First World War 1914–18.

Key dates

1884	Creation of the Social Democratic Federation
	Creation of the Fabian Society
	Creation of the Socialist League
1893	Creation of the Independent Labour Party
1900	Setting up of the Labour Representation Committee (LRC)
1903	Electoral pact agreed between the LRC and the Liberal Party
1906	LRC wins 29 seats in the general election
	Foundation of the Labour Party
1906–9	Labour supports Liberal reforms
1910	Labour loses seats in January general election
1911–13	Industrial unrest
1915	Arthur Henderson, the leader of the Labour Party, joins the Coalition Cabinet
1916	Henderson joins Lloyd George's War Cabinet – a number of Labour MPs become junior ministers
1917	Henderson resigns and is replaced by a former Labour leader, George Barnes
1918	New Labour Party Constitution is approved

1 | The Origins of the Labour Party 1895–1906

Key question
Why did a Labour
Party develop in this
period?

The immediate origins of the Labour Party before 1895 are to be found in the 1880s in the development of what some historians have termed the 'Socialist Revival'. This term describes a renewed interest in the principles of socialism that was marked by the founding of political groups dedicated in general to socialist ideas.

During the 1840s the working-class political movement known as the Chartists had emerged demanding political rights for all adult men and arguing for a fairer distribution of wealth. Not all Chartists were socialists but the movement unquestionably embraced some of the principles of socialism. With the collapse of Chartism in the late 1840s, however, and the onset of better social conditions in the 1850s, the steam went out of both working-class political protest in general and the appeal of socialist principles. However, by the 1880s socialism and the idea that British politics needed a separate working-class political party that would promote the ideas of socialism were very much back under discussion. The reasons for this were as follows:

- The ideas of Karl Marx as outlined in his work *Capital* published in 1867 were attracting some attention. Originally written in German and entitled *Das Kapital*, *Capital* was translated into English in the 1870s. Marx was a German revolutionary, who advanced the idea that human society operated according to scientific principles. Just as the physical universe was governed by the laws of chemistry and physics so, too, the behaviour of human beings was determined by social laws. These could be scientifically studied and applied. Marx claimed that the critical determinant of human behaviour was **class struggle**, a process that operated throughout history.
- From around 1870, a series of economic slumps hit some sections of the working classes severely.
- In 1867 a Reform Act meant that more working-class men were able to vote.
- Although the material conditions of the working classes were generally improving, the gap between them and the middle and upper classes continued to increase.
- Although both the Liberal Party and the Conservatives tried to appeal to the working classes there was no real scope for working-class participation in either party. The Liberal Party claimed to be the natural party of the working classes but working-class men found it difficult to be accepted as prospective MPs for the Party.

Key term
Class struggle
A continuing conflict at every stage of history between those who possessed economic and political power and those who did not, in simple terms the 'haves' and the 'have-nots'.

The formation of political groups

In 1884 three separate groups were formed to push for greater working-class participation in the political system.

The SDF

The Social Democratic Federation (SDF) was a **Marxist** group that aimed to promote class hostility and an eventual revolution to take over political power. It was founded by an ex-Tory, Eton-educated stockbroker, H.M. Hyndman, who converted to Marxism after reading *Das Kapital*.

The Fabians

The Fabians were a small middle-class group of intellectuals who favoured working towards socialism gradually through the existing parliamentary system. They took their name from the Roman general Fabius Maximus, who was known for his cautious approach to military conflict, preferring patient sieges to bloody head-on battles. Playwright George Bernard Shaw was a founder member, along with a civil servant, Sidney Webb, and his wife Beatrice. Sidney Webb eventually went on to write the influential *Labour and the New Social Order* (1918) and inspire the Labour Party's revised constitution in the same year (see page 98).

The Socialist League

The Socialist League was initially an offshoot of the SDF. It was founded by William Morris, who differed from Hyndman in his view of the nature of a future socialist society. Essentially however the group was Marxist in tone and Morris agreed with Hyndman that a revolution was the only way to bring about socialism.

The ILP

The 1880s and 1890s was a time of increasing economic difficulty with unemployment and hardship causing serious unrest. In 1886, during a severe winter, an SDF open-air meeting to protest about unemployment turned into a riot. In November 1887, Trafalgar Square in the centre of London was taken over by groups of the unemployed. When the police baton-charged the demonstrators, over 200 people were injured.

In 1893 the Independent Labour Party (ILP) was formed. Its founder was James Keir Hardie. It was based on three important sources of influence:

- **Radical liberalism**, which found the traditional Liberal Party too conservative and capitalist based.
- Trade unionism, which was becoming increasingly political.
- Nonconformity, which was coming increasingly to link Christianity with politics. As Keir Hardie, himself a strong Nonconformist, put it, 'the final goal of socialism is a form of social economy, very strongly akin to the principles set forth in the Sermon on the Mount.'

The ILP was formed as a national organisation out of 'Labour' groups that had been springing up around the country. In 1894 it gained an important recruit in James Ramsay MacDonald, a warehouse clerk, who had turned to journalism and who would go on the become the first Labour Prime Minister in 1924. However, it is important not to exaggerate the impact of the ILP. Its strength was limited to particular areas and its peak membership in 1895 was 35,000. In 1895, it put up 28 candidates at the general election though none was elected.

Profile: James Keir Hardie 1856–1915

1856 – Born in Lanarkshire
1886 – Became Secretary of the Scottish Miners' Federation
1892 – Became an MP
1893 – Founded the ILP
1900 – Helped to set up the LRC
1906 – Became chairman of the Labour Party
1914 – Retired from being chairman of the Labour Party
1915 – Died

Background and early career

Hardie was born in Lanarkshire, Scotland, in 1856 and originally worked in the mines from the age of seven until he was 24 years old. Largely self-educated he escaped the life of a miner through trade union work, becoming Secretary of the Scottish Miners' Federation in 1886. He became a journalist, founding and editing *The Labour Leader*. In 1892 he became the MP for the Welsh mining constituency of Merthyr Tydfil. The following year he founded the Independent Labour Party (ILP), and became its leader.

Later career

In 1895 Hardie was defeated in the general election but in 1900 he was re-elected at Merthyr Tydfil. In 1900 he played a major role in setting up the Labour Representation Committee and became its leader. Once the Labour Party officially formed in 1906 he became its first chairman and in effect its leader.

As leader he championed many ideas that were not always widely popular. He was a committed Christian, a Nonconformist with uncompromising views about alcohol, which he regarded as an evil influence on working-class self-improvement. He was a strong enthusiast for education at a time when many working-class activists and trade unionists saw it as an irrelevance. He was also an outspoken advocate of the right of women to vote and women's rights in general. He was not a particularly skilful politician in terms of diplomacy. He often failed to see that being less outspoken might help win over opponents gradually.

When the First World War broke out in 1914, his pacifist views left him with no option but to retire from his leading position in the Party. He died in 1915, his health having been broken by his distress at the war. Although he died too soon to serve in any high office, it is not unreasonable to regard him as having done more than any other individual, by the time of his death, to make the Labour Party a credible force in British politics.

The creation of the LRC

The single most important development in the formation of the Labour Party came in 1900 and it was the trade unions who sponsored it. Angered by increasing aggression on the part of employers in the tough economic climate of the 1890s the trade unions decided that more direct political action was needed.

At the Trades Union Congress (TUC) annual conference of 1899 the railwaymen's union put forward a resolution that a further conference should be held for the purpose of 'securing a better representation of the interests of labour in the House of Commons'. A clear, if not overwhelming, majority carried the resolution. Accordingly 129 delegates assembled in London in February 1900.

The TUC, inexperienced in political action, invited the SDF, the Fabians and the ILP to send delegates. The ILP took the lead. Recognising the basic conservatism of the trade unions, Hardie steered the delegates away from the firebrand politics of the SDF, while at the same time blocking the idea that some trade unionists had that working-class MPs, once elected, should confine themselves to particular 'labour issues' only.

A committee was established to work towards the formation of a 'distinct Labour group in Parliament who shall have their own **whips** and agree upon their own policy'. Hardie hoped to call the new organisation the 'United Labour Party' but this was considered too controversial and in the end the conference agreed on the title 'Labour Representation Committee' (LRC) as safer. It was, however, the foundation of the Labour Party in everything but name.

LRC support

From the start, the new organisation was determined to put political realities ahead of ideology. Fearful that the term 'socialist' was too radical in its implications, and aware that the trade unions were not entirely comfortable with it, the LRC began to use the term 'socialistic', meaning broadly sympathetic to socialist ideas, but not rigidly committed to doctrines such as state ownership.

Moreover the LRC was open to active collaboration with outside groups, not least the Liberal Party. An electoral pact was agreed between them in 1903. This was an agreement to avoid running candidates against each other in constituencies where a split vote between them might result in the election of a Conservative candidate (see page 36).

The LRC received a huge, if in some ways unwelcome, boost in 1901 in the form of the Taff Vale judgement. The railwaymen's union, the Amalgamated Society of Railway Servants, had called strikes to try to force the employers to grant formal recognition of the union. In response the Taff Vale Railway Company sued the union for damages. On appeal, the House of Lords found in favour of the employers and awarded substantial damages plus costs against the union. This sent shock waves through the trade

Key question
Why was the LRC formed in 1900?

Key term

Whips
MPs who within their own political party, ensure that the other MPs vote according to the wishes of the party leadership. If the party is in government, the whips are paid members of the government.

Key dates

Setting up of the Labour Representation Committee (LRC): 1900

Electoral pact agreed between the LRC and the Liberal Party: 1903

Key date

LRC wins 29 seats in the general election: 1906

unions as a whole. Previously cautious and sceptical unions who had steered away from involvement with the LRC were converted. A total of 127 unions joined the LRC as a direct result of the Taff Vale verdict, lifting total membership from 353,000 to 847,000. The unions levied the members for funds to support the LRC and it was able to secure the election of 29 MPs at the 1906 general election.

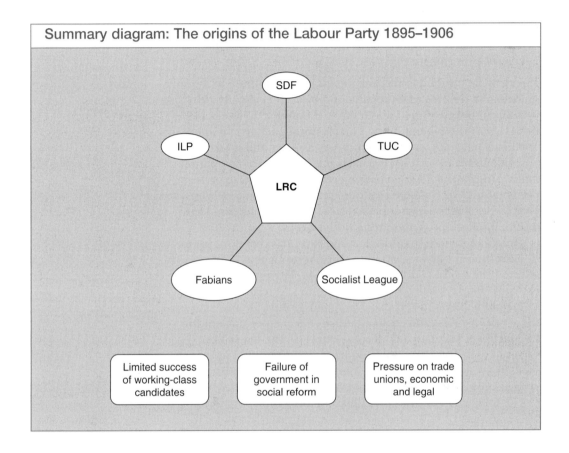

Summary diagram: The origins of the Labour Party 1895–1906

SDF

ILP   TUC

LRC

Fabians   Socialist League

Limited success of working-class candidates

Failure of government in social reform

Pressure on trade unions, economic and legal

Key question
How important was the role of the Labour Party in 1906–14?

2 | The Labour Party in the Commons 1906–14

The title 'Labour Party' was formally adopted in 1906. Following the general election the MPs elected as LRC candidates, Miners' Union candidates and Independents (in effect, all those sitting specifically to represent working-class interests) informally agreed to act as a single parliamentary party. Even so, the Miners did not officially merge with the Labour Party until 1908 and when they did so it was seen as marking a clear change in the political weight of the party.

Key date

Foundation of the Labour Party by uniting LRC, Miners' MPs and Independent Labour MPs in the House of Commons: 1906

The 1906–10 Parliament

The extent of the influence of the Labour Party in the Parliament of 1906–10 is controversial:

- **'Labour' historians** tend to emphasise the importance of the Labour Party by suggesting that it encouraged or even forced the Liberals to adopt policies directly favourable to the working class.
- **'Marxist' historians** see the Party as abandoning socialist principles and collaborating with the capitalist employers.
- Other historians argue that the Party was not strong enough to have any decisive influence on the decisions taken by the Liberal Government.

It is clear that the Liberal Government was committed to a policy of extensive reforms when it came to power. It is equally clear that the official policy of the Labour Party differed little in essence from that of the Liberal Party. The electoral pact arrangement of 1903 (see page 36), even though it was a secret and informal agreement, meant that both parties had to produce compatible manifestos for the 1906 general election. These had to be designed to be acceptable to a range of potential voters, who, in vital constituencies were expected to support a candidate who would, in effect, be representing both parties.

The subsequent role of the Labour Party has therefore been discussed primarily in relation to those reforms that most directly affected the interests of the working class. The problem with this is that so much of the Liberals' legislation was centred on the welfare of vulnerable and disadvantaged groups. In assessing these reforms it is difficult to establish that the presence of the Labour Party MPs had any decisive effect on the legislation involved. The fact that they supported it, encouraged it or even took a part in its formulation is not in itself evidence that such reforms would not have taken place without them.

The following key examples illustrate the point.

The Trades Disputes Act 1906

This Act is often seen as direct evidence for the influence of the Labour Party since it changed the law to protect trade unions involved in strike action from being sued for damages by employers, i.e. it reversed the Taff Vale verdict of 1901 (see pages 90–1). However, it is important to remember that the need for a change in the law had been accepted by both the Liberal Party and the Unionist Party in the years after 1901. The Balfour government initially rejected calls for a change in the law but then had a rethink and set up a Royal Commission to look into the issue. The only doubt thereafter was whether the law should be reformed to allow full or only partial protection for union funds. The Liberal Prime Minister Campbell-Bannerman favoured full protection.

Despite this, owing to the concerns of other Cabinet ministers, the Liberal Government originally proposed a bill offering partial immunity for unions. The Labour Party countered this with its

Labour historians
Historians who generally see the rise of the Labour Party as an inevitable (and welcome) process.

Marxist historians
Historians who accept Marx's view that political and social evolution towards a Communist society is inevitable.

own bill offering full immunity. Campbell-Bannerman, entirely on his own initiative, then committed the government to accepting the Labour version, which totally accorded with his own view and indeed the views of many Liberal backbenchers who had actually championed such an option during the general election campaign.

The Education (Provision of Meals) Act 1906

The momentum for this measure, which gave direct aid for malnourished schoolchildren, was much greater before 1906 than is generally acknowledged. The Balfour Government, responding to pressure inside and outside Parliament, had issued an order for 'destitute' schoolchildren to be fed through the Poor Law, but this proved difficult to administer. In any case the term 'destitute' strictly only covered those children who were totally without means of support.

The Liberals favoured direct legislation to address the problem, but had not devised a specific proposal at the time of the 1906 general election. When a newly elected Labour MP brought forward a Private Member's Bill authorising Local Education Authorities to feed 'needy' children using rate money, the Liberal Government seized on the proposal and made it government policy. This was a Labour initiative most certainly, but was hardly imposed on the government.

Key question
What led to the Party's decline in political power?

Divisions in the Labour Party

The picture that therefore emerges tends to support the view that while the Labour Party did try to put pressure on the Liberal Government between 1906 and 1910, the government's responses were dictated by its own agenda. This picture is reinforced by the fact that the Labour Party itself was a broadly based organisation with no clear commitment to a full programme of socialism. In 1908, Ben Tillett, a member of the Independent Labour Party, which still maintained a separate identity within the Party as a whole, published a pamphlet entitled *Is the Parliamentary Labour Party a Failure?* which criticised the moderate line the party was adopting. This was followed up in 1910 by an even more critical, alternative election manifesto, put forward by the ILP, entitled 'Let us Reform the Labour Party', which called for a shared platform with the Marxist Social Democratic Federation.

Divisions in the Labour Party ran deep. Issues such as the female suffrage created significant problems. The idea of women voting was not popular among many trade unionists. Working-class men were generally among the least sympathetic elements to the idea. Hostility towards the militant suffragettes was probably greater among these groups than any other. However, the more committed socialists (especially Keir Hardie of the ILP) were passionately committed to the cause of women's suffrage. In the general election of 1906, serious disputes arose in some constituencies over whether LRC candidates should accept help from suffragette activists in their election campaigns.

What message is this cartoon projecting? How accurate is its representation of the relationship between Liberalism and Labour?

FORCED FELLOWSHIP.

SUSPICIOUS-LOOKING PARTY. "ANY OBJECTION TO MY COMPANY, GUV'NOR? I'M AGOIN' YOUR WAY"—(*aside*) "AND FURTHER."

The 1910 general elections

From 1910 the situation at Westminster changed dramatically and the change did not favour the position of the Labour Party. In the general election of January 1910 the Labour Party fielded only 70 candidates. This was partly the result of fears about financial problems resulting from the Osborne Judgement of 1909, which had made trade union contribution to political parties illegal. The Osborne Judgement was reversed in 1913 by the Trade Union Act, but in the meantime the Labour Party faced a cash-flow crisis. The result of the election was that 40 Labour MPs were elected – all from constituencies where no Liberal candidate had stood. This rose by two in the second general election that year, but Labour had still fallen back in strength from 1906.

Thereafter, between 1910 and 1914, Labour candidates failed to hold seats in a series of by-elections so that by 1914 the Party had only 36 MPs.

Labour loses seats in January general election: 1910

Key date

Perhaps even more serious in some ways for the Labour Party was the ending of the Liberal Party's overall majority. Before 1910, the Liberal Government had enjoyed more or less complete freedom of action in terms of developing its policies. The emergence of 'New Liberalism' (see pages 29–31) made many in the Liberal Party sympathetic to those they regarded as natural allies. However, from 1910, the Irish National Party held the balance of power in the House of Commons. Twice the size of the Labour Party in terms of MPs, it could now exercise a more decisive pressure on the Liberal Government than the Labour Party had ever done.

The new emphasis of Liberal–INP relations on House of Lords reform and Irish Home Rule moved the political focus away from the natural concerns of the Labour Party. The extent of the Liberal reforms up to 1911 had in any case reduced the urgency of many of the issues that had united Liberals and Labour in 1906. On the eve of the First World War, despite the fact that the Party was making encouraging progress in local elections and securing influence or even overall control in some local authorities, the future of the Labour Party seemed far from assured.

Key question
Why was there so much industrial unrest during this period?

3 | The Trade Unions and Industrial Unrest 1910–14

The years between 1910 and the outbreak of the First World War in 1914 saw a huge increase in trade union membership from 2.5 million to 4 million. This was a trend that would continue strongly during the war and into the post-war period. The period from 1910 to 1914 was also marked by a wave of strikes. The increased militancy can be attributed to the following factors:

Key term

Real wages
Define the value of goods or services that wages can actually buy. For example, if wages remain the same while food prices increase, their 'real' value has gone down. On the other hand if food prices fall the 'real' value of wages has risen.

- From around 1900 the value of **real wages** was gradually falling owing to increases in the cost of living.
- From 1910 there was a fall in the levels of unemployment which made many workers more willing to confront the employers.
- Prices rose particularly steeply in 1911–12.
- The middle and upper classes were actually improving their position, leading to increased bitterness among the workers whose living standards had worsened.

Strikes 1910–13

1910
The first major confrontation came in the south Wales coalfield in the autumn of 1910. A dispute arose over payments for miners working difficult seams of coal. Militancy had been on the increase in south Wales for a number of years and the general mood of bitterness soon resulted in a rash of strikes. It was not long before confrontations between strikers and the authorities produced violence.

1911

During rioting in Tonypandy in south Wales in 1911, a man died from injuries he had sustained in a fight with local police officers and many others suffered less serious injuries. The Home Secretary, Winston Churchill, felt that the seriousness of the situation required that army units be drafted in to support the local police. This decision elevated the Tonypandy riots to mythological status in working-class history. The wave of strikes went on for 10 months before ending in defeat for the miners. This, however, was only the start of the unrest.

In June 1911, the Seamen's Union went on strike and the dockers and railwaymen came out on strike in sympathy. Two months later, two strikers were shot dead by troops in Liverpool after a general riot had broken out. In the same week, troops shot dead two men who were part of a crowd attacking a train at Llanelli.

1912

In 1912, the first national pit strike began, lasting from February until April, with the miners demanding a national minimum wage. The government responded to this, with a compromise, by passing the Minimum Wage Act for Mining, which set up local boards in colliery districts to fix minimum wages for miners working on difficult seams. In the same year there were also strikes in the London docks and among transport workers.

1913

In 1913 there were strikes in the metal-working industries of the Midlands and a major strike of transport workers in Dublin.

The sheer numbers of people involved in these industrial disputes was unprecedented. From the late 1890s onwards, more and more unskilled workers had been drawn into trade unionism. By 1910 around 17 per cent of workers were in trade unions, and the unrest encouraged the trend. By 1914 the figure had risen to 25 per cent.

The rise in female membership of unions was the most remarkable feature of the period. In 1904 there were 126,000 women trade union members. By 1913 there were 431,000, making up 10 per cent of all trade unionists.

4 | The Labour Party and the First World War 1914–18

Key question
How did the Labour Party react to the outbreak of the war?

The outbreak of war in 1914 appeared to threaten to the future of the Labour Party. However, in many ways, the war became the making of the Party as a credible alternative government in British politics. The initial danger came from the very serious divisions in the Party over how it should respond to the war. Whereas the Conservatives and the Irish National Party pledged themselves to the full support of the Liberal Government in the war effort, the Labour Party faced an internal dispute over policy. There were three main factions.

- A 'patriotic' element in the Party argued that war meant that all previous political and class hostilities should be put aside and the Labour movement as a whole, i.e. including the trade unions, should wholeheartedly support the war effort.
- A 'moderate' group argued for more conditional support with a more critical approach when needed to protect working-class interests.
- A 'radical' Marxist-inspired element demanded that the war be condemned as an imperialist conspiracy by collapsing capitalist nations.

These divisions were further complicated by the moral concerns of individuals in the Party who held 'pacifist' views. From their perspective, war itself was morally wrong and could not be supported. Some individual Liberals also held to this view, for example John Morley resigned from his position because he felt he could not serve in a government at war.

From the earliest stages of the war, elements in the Labour Party campaigned vigorously against '**militarism**' – often in the face of public hostility. The most immediate outcome of the war in 1914 for the Labour Party was the resignation of Ramsay MacDonald as leader. MacDonald felt he could not support the war and resigned as a consequence. In September 1914 he helped form a new group, the Union of Democratic Control (UDC), which aimed to maintain the arguments of those who opposed entry into the war and continue the demand for settlement by negotiation and not military victory. MacDonald was replaced as Labour Party leader by Arthur Henderson.

Key term	
Militarism Principle that military power is a desirable end in itself and that its use to achieve objectives is desirable.	

Key question	
How did the First World War change the fortunes of the Labour Party?	

Key dates	
Arthur Henderson, the Leader of the Labour Party, joins the Coalition Cabinet: 1915	
Henderson joins Lloyd George's War Cabinet – a number of Labour MPs become junior ministers: 1916	

Coalition government

In early 1915 a scandal was brewing at the highest level as a result of the failure of the Liberal Government to provide sufficient munitions for the war effort. The attitude of Asquith's government at the start of the war had been to insist that the war could be fought on the basis of 'business as usual'. By the spring of 1915 this policy had so restricted the war effort on the Western Front that the Unionists refused to continue supporting the government unless something was done.

As a result, Asquith agreed to the formation of a coalition government of national unity. Since the co-operation of the trade unions was essential to the war effort, Henderson, as leader of the Labour Party, was invited to join the Cabinet, nominally to take charge of education, but in fact to be the representative of 'labour' interests. Other Labour leaders were brought into the government at more junior levels. When the Lloyd George coalition was formed in 1916, Henderson continued in the new 'War Cabinet' as one of only five members. Labour had arrived on the governmental scene.

In 1916, Henderson became involved in a dispute with his Cabinet colleagues. Following the Russian Revolution in March 1917 that overthrew the Tsar, the new Russian Government suggested a new set of war aims based on 'no **annexations** and no **indemnities**'.

Henderson went to Russia in May 1917 on behalf of the Cabinet and he returned convinced that the Russian war aims must be adopted by the Labour Party. He also wanted to send delegates to a socialist conference being organised in Sweden at which there would be representatives from socialist parties on both sides in the war as well as neutrals. Lloyd George at first agreed to this, but then faced with protests from the French, who wanted both territory and compensation from the Germans after the war, he changed his mind.

Henderson refused to back down and resigned from the War Cabinet. He was replaced by George Barnes, another former Labour Party leader. The other Labour ministers in the government all remained in office.

End of the war 1918

As the war drew to a close the Labour Party began to heal the divisions that had been caused in its own ranks. In 1918, Sidney Webb, one of the original Fabians and now a leading party figure, drafted 'Labour and the New Social Order', a clear party programme with a strongly socialist tone. It was the basis for a new constitution for the Party, the fourth clause of which promised extensive state control of the economy in the interests of 'the producers by hand and by brain' of the nation's wealth.

The foreign policy of the Party was provided by bringing in the UDC. This marked the return of MacDonald as the unacknowledged joint leader of the Party with Henderson and also the beginning of the end of Labour's association with the coalition.

Once the war was over, a Labour Party conference was called for 14 November, just three days after the armistice. Lloyd George had already called a general election and he urged the Labour Party to continue as part of the coalition. At the conference the Fabian George Bernard Shaw famously urged that the Party 'Go back to Lloyd George and say – nothing doing'. Most of the Labour ministers did precisely this and resigned. The few that did not, resigned from the Labour Party.

Labour then went on to fight the general election as the only party of undivided opposition to the coalition government. There was a price to pay for this show of independence. Despite a franchise that now included all men and most women over 30, Labour did not achieve a major breakthrough. In all, the Party won 59 seats and all but one of them were trade union sponsored. The 'pacifists' were shown what the electorate thought of them when almost all of them lost their seats.

MacDonald was defeated as was Henderson, who had served at Cabinet level. But the die was now cast. Independence from Lloyd George gave Labour a united platform denied to the Liberals, who were hopelessly divided and demoralised. The new constitution of 1918 meant that the Labour Party had a programme that could

Key terms

Annexations
Territory taken by the winner from the loser.

Indemnities
Compensation paid by the losers to the winners to cover, partly or in full, their war costs. The term 'reparations' is often used to describe this.

Key date

Henderson resigns and is replaced by a former Labour leader, George Barnes: 1917

New Labour Party Constitution is approved: 1918

offer the voters in the now virtually democratised political system (where over 20 million people could vote) relevant reforms and the vision of a socialist future.

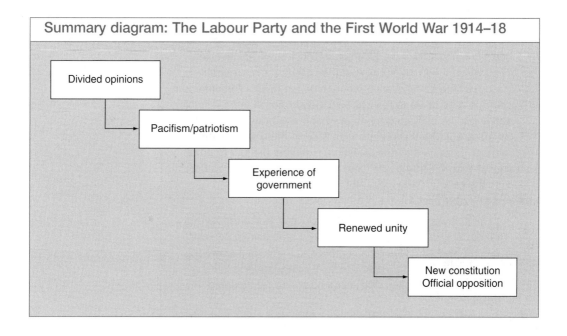

Summary diagram: The Labour Party and the First World War 1914–18

Divided opinions

Pacifism/patriotism

Experience of government

Renewed unity

New constitution
Official opposition

Study Guide: AS Questions

In the style of AQA

Read the following source and then answer the questions that follow.

Adapted from: British Political History, 1867–1990, *by Malcolm Pearce and Geoffrey Stewart.*

On the surface the Labour movement seemed far from successful by 1914. It had emerged but was overshadowed by the Liberals in parliament and was troubled by trade union activity. This is, however, too bleak a picture.

(a) Using the source and your own knowledge, comment on 'overshadowed by the Liberals in parliament' in the context of the Labour movement from 1906–1914. (3 marks)
(b) Explain how trade union activity both helped and hindered the emerging Labour Party between 1900 and 1914. (7 marks)
(c) Had the Labour Party established itself as a major political force by 1914? Explain your answer. (15 marks)

Source: AQA, May 2002

Exam tips

The cross-references are intended to take you straight to the material that will help you to answer the questions.

(a) The source is a prompt and offers nothing beyond the bare quote – this is not atypical of the question type. Your own knowledge should tell you that the comment refers to the overwhelming size of the Liberals' majority between 1906 and 1910 which made the support of the Labour Party irrelevant to the government's legislative programme (page 92). The comment could also be taken to refer to the Liberals' social reforms, which seemed to be delivering much of what the Labour Party stood for (page 95). For the later period 1910–14 the Liberals were focused more on the Irish Question, reflecting the fact that the loss of their majority made them dependent on the INP rather than the Labour Party (page 95).

(b) It is probably best to take this chronologically.

- In 1900 it was the initiative of the TUC that led to the setting up of the LRC and the emergence of a real drive to achieve greater working-class representation in Parliament (page 90).
- The trade unions delivered potential voters and the funding that enabled a proper election campaign to be mounted in 1906.
- A significant number of the Labour MPs who came together in Parliament after 1906 were union affiliates, most noticeably of the Miners' Union (page 91).
- However, trade union support came at a price. Labour policy was affected by the unions' pressure on some issues such as the women's suffrage question, to which many trade unionists were unsympathetic (pages 75–6).
- The Osborne Judgement in 1909 showed the vulnerability of Labour in its financial dependence on subscriptions from the unions (page 94).
- In 1910–13 the period of labour unrest saw some violent confrontations from which the Labour Party wished to distance itself while at the same time fearing the possible backlash (pages 95–6).

(c) The key here is to reach a clear judgement. You need to balance your assessment between the obvious lack of progress in Parliament and the wider picture of the build-up of the Party's infrastructure in the country at grass-roots level.

- By 1914 Labour had been losing by-elections over the past three years and had only 36 MPs, which compares unfavourably with the 52 who came together in 1906 (page 94).
- The Party had also suffered from the effect of the Osborne Judgement, which had cut off its funding from the unions since 1909 (page 94).
- However, this was subsequently reversed by the Liberals in the Trade Union Act of 1913, and the independence of Labour

MPs had been helped by the introduction of salaries for MPs in 1911.
- Labour's performance in local elections was also encouraging. Overall, it is most likely that Labour in 1914 represented a party with the potential to be a major force in the future, rather than an actual major force at that time.

In the style of Edexcel

In what ways did the outcome of the elections of 1910 affect the relationships between the Liberals and other political parties?

(30 marks)

Source: Edexcel, January 2003

Exam tips

The cross-references are intended to take you straight to the material that will help you to answer the questions.

Make sure that you follow the standard requirement for this type of question and offer comment on the relative importance of the various factors and try to establish linkages between them. Categorising factors is another way to gain high marks and a good way to establish links between them.

In this question:
- The key effects stemmed from the loss of the Liberals' overall majority in January 1910 – the second election at the end of the year produced more or less the same outcome (pages 94–5).
- The main effect was to make the Liberals dependent on the Irish National Party, which had over 80 MPs. The consequence of this was that Home Rule became an immediate policy for action rather than something that the Liberals were pledged to, but reluctant to attempt. The Irish had been lukewarm on some aspects of the 1909 Budget so their support was now vital (pages 113–14).
- The revival of the Home Rule issue meant relations between the Liberals and the Conservatives were on a collision course since Home Rule could not be attempted meaningfully without first bringing in reform of the House of Lords to remove or limit its power of veto (pages 72–4).
- At the same time the Labour Party can be seen as less influential. It lost seats overall and was irrelevant to the debate about Ireland and reform of the House of Lords since which ever way it voted it could not decisively affect the outcome (page 94). In practice, the Labour Party approved of the reform of the Lords and did not oppose Irish Home Rule so it was effectively sidelined.

In the style of OCR

Study the four sources on the impact of the First World War on the Labour Party, and then answer all the sub-questions.

(a) Study Sources B and C
Compare these sources as evidence for differences in attitudes in the years 1916–18 to Labour's involvement in coalition government.   (20 marks)
(b) Study all the sources
Using all these sources and your own knowledge, assess the view that it was the impact of the First World War that did most to establish Labour as a 'strong and independent' party.
(40 marks)

Source: OCR, January 2003

Source A

From: Beatrice Webb, Diary, January 1916. A socialist and leading member of the Fabian Society describes Labour's divisions over the Military Service Bill introduced to the House of Commons on 6 January 1916.

The year opens badly for Labour. The Munitions Act, the Defence of the Realm Act and the suppression of a free press have been followed by the Cabinet's decision in favour of compulsory military service. The next step will be the conscription of the whole of industry; the 'servile state' will soon be established. Nearly all Labour MPs were converted to some measure of conscription. Henderson, the Labour leader, said that the alternative was a general election, and that every Labour MP who was against conscription would lose their seat in such an election.

Source B

The same left-wing Labour supporter takes a fairly critical view of the Labour Party's decision to accept office in the new coalition government led by David Lloyd George.

The meeting decided by eighteen votes to twelve in favour of accepting office. It is very difficult to know what these Labour leaders were thinking. Although beating of the Germans may have passed through their minds. But their main mistake was the illusion that the mere presence of Labour men in the Government is a sign of democratic progress. Each thinks he will get the policies he wants. They do not realize that, when they serve with experienced officials, they are no longer independent.

Source C

From: Sidney Webb, Address to his Constituents, reprinted in the magazine The New Statesman, *November 1918. The husband of Beatrice Webb, and one of those chiefly responsible for drawing up Labour's policies, explains why the Labour Party should fight alone in the coming 1918 general election.*

There were good reasons for Labour joining a coalition ministry: as long as the War was the dominant issue, on which all were agreed as to policy. But now is proposed to have a peace-time coalition. It is clear that the other parties are not prepared to adopt our policies of reconstruction, as worked out by Labour during the last two years. Therefore, in the General Election, the policies of each party should be submitted separately to the electorate for its decision. Labour is prepared to do this. Besides, in a time of industrial unrest, the best safeguard of democracy would be a strong and independent Labour party in Parliament.

Source D

From: R. McKibben, The Evolution of the Labour Party 1910–24, *1973. A modern historian comments on the fortunes of the Labour and Liberal Parties in the early years of the twentieth century.*

The rise of the Labour party and the slow wearing down of the Liberal party both came from a developing sense of common aims and interests by the working class. This process was well under way by 1914 and would have continued, with or without the War. The War did have a significant effect in bringing about the 1918 Representation of the People Act, which gave electorate voted Labour in 1918; but, had it been given the vote earlier, it would probably have done the same in 1914.

Exam tips

(a) Sources B and C both come from highly placed figures in the Labour Party and as such offer a valuable insight into the attitudes towards participation in government. Both sources draw out the imperative issue of the war: even the criticism of Beatrice Webb accepts that this was an important factor, and she also draws attention to the idea that merely by being members of the government the cause of democracy was being served (though she concludes that this was an illusion). Source C is quite compatible in some ways with Source B in that it is looking to what is best for democracy and concluding that in the changed circumstances of 1918 collaboration is no longer acceptable.

(b) This requires a balanced judgement based on consideration of the impact of the war on the Labour Party. To do this properly you will need to refer to the pre-war period in some detail; your own knowledge will need to be secure, as only Source D refers in any way to the period before 1914 and this only in very general terms. As always with this type of question, you need to group the sources according to what they say and construct a thematic answer. Use the sources as fully as possible and make sure that you refer to all of them. Look for opportunities to use your own knowledge to elaborate on the detail in the sources as well as using it to bring out points that the sources do not cover. Some kind of judgement on the state of the Party in 1914 is vital, as well as a balanced coverage of both the negative and positive impacts of the war, e.g. divisions of opinion and experience of administration.

In the style of WJEC

How far were the Liberals influenced by the growth of the Labour Party in the period 1900–1914?

Exam tips

The cross-references are intended to take you straight to the material that will help you to answer the question.

This is an evaluative essay in which you need to balance the argument using evidence to support the idea that the growth of the Labour Party did influence the Liberals in the period, against the evidence to the contrary. You should discuss:

- The impact of the electoral pact and what it suggests about the relationship (page 36).
- The joint manifesto for the 1906 general election and the nature of its content (page 92).
- The actual legislation introduced by the Liberals and the extent to which it can be said to derive from Labour (pages 92–3).
- The scale of the Labour Party's electoral performance (page 94).
- The Liberals' majority to 1910 and the impact of its loss (page 130).
- The position of Labour from 1910 to 1914 (pages 94–5).

WJEC awards marks separately for content (one-third) and approach (two-thirds) to make up the total mark, so make sure that you explain and support your arguments with appropriate detail.

6 Ireland 1895–1918

POINTS TO CONSIDER

The relationship between Ireland and the British mainland has been a key theme in the history of the British Isles. Domination by mainland Britain has had a massive impact on the course of Irish history. Equally, however, events in and issues relating to Ireland have frequently had a major impact on British politics. In this chapter, Irish affairs will be examined in two stages:

- The origins and nature of the Irish Question
- An analysis of the events between 1895 and 1918 considering:
  - The revival of political nationalism
  - The impact of the constitutional crisis 1909–11
  - The Third Home Rule Bill 1912
  - The First World War 1914–18.

Key dates

1800	Act of Union
1845–51	The potato famine hits Ireland
1869	Irish Anglican Church disestablished
1870	Land Act gives Irish tenants limited rights
1882	Second Irish Land Act extends tenant rights
1886	Gladstone introduces the Home Rule Bill for Ireland, which fails to become law
1892–3	Gladstone's second attempt at Home Rule for Ireland also fails
1910	Irish National Party holds balance of power in the House of Commons
1911	Parliament Act
1912	Third Home Rule Bill introduced
1912–13	The Ulster Crisis – Ireland on brink of civil war over issue of Home Rule
1914	Third Home Rule Bill passed but suspended for the duration of the war
1916	Easter Rising – Irish independence proclaimed but rebels defeated and leaders executed
1918	Sinn Fein Nationalist Party wins majority of Irish seats and declares Ireland independent from Great Britain

Key question
What was the Easter Rising?

1 | The Origins and Nature of the Irish Question

In 1895 the relationship between Ireland and Great Britain was probably more stable than it had been at any time during the nineteenth century. The immediate history of the Irish Question over the course of the century can be summarised as follows:

- In 1800 the Act of Union constitutionally united Ireland with the rest of Great Britain. This created a 'United Kingdom of Great Britain and Ireland'.

- Under the Act of Union, Ireland's separate parliament was abolished and Irish MPs were elected directly to the House of Commons at Westminster. A limited number of Irish Peers were also admitted to the House of Lords.

- Although Ireland was a predominantly Roman Catholic country, the Anglican church was established as the official state Church in Ireland. This was a source of constant resentment until, in 1869, during Gladstone's first government, the Anglican Church was 'disestablished', putting it on the same status as other Churches in Ireland.

- In the period 1845–51 Ireland had suffered from the potato blight that destroyed potato crops all over Europe. However, in Ireland the poverty stricken peasantry depended very heavily and sometimes almost entirely on potatoes as their main source of food. As a result around one million people in Ireland died of starvation and related diseases, while around two million emigrated. Great Britain failed to take any effective action to combat this 'potato famine' and the anger it produced in Ireland was passed down the generations.

- The central social problem in Ireland was the depressed economic condition of the rural peasant farmers. They farmed land that was often owned by English landlords, many of whom lived permanently in England. Their impoverished Catholic tenants mostly had no security in their tenancy agreements and could be vulnerable to eviction. Farming methods were primitive and unproductive compared to England. Gladstone went a long way towards solving the land problem with two acts in 1870 and 1882 which, taken together, had the effect of giving tenants proper tenancy rights, protection from unfair rents and the right to sell on their tenancy as a business.

- In order to 'kill Home Rule with kindness' the Conservative Government of Lord Salisbury (1886–92) followed a policy of allowing loans to tenant farmers who wished to buy out their landlords. The hope was that over a period of time the hated 'absentee' landlords would disappear and a new class of conservative-minded Catholic farmers would emerge.

- The problem still remained of the constitutional relationship between Great Britain and Ireland. In the second half of the nineteenth century a **republican** group known as the Irish Republican Brotherhood emerged demanding independence.

Key term

Republican
One who rejects the principle of monarchy in favour of a head of state elected by or appointed from the people of the country.

This group was prepared to use violence to advance its campaign but it commanded little support in Ireland. More moderate Irish nationalists, who had formed an Irish National Party to put Ireland's case at Westminster, demanded 'Home Rule' for Ireland. This would have meant that Ireland could assume control over its own internal affairs but not for matters such as foreign affairs or trade. It was this demand that Gladstone agreed to in 1886 and 1892 with his two Home Rule bills. Both bills, however, were defeated in Parliament.

- The decision to offer Ireland Home Rule in 1886 exposed the so-called 'Ulster Problem'. The northern counties of Ireland, collectively known as Ulster, were populated by a predominant majority of Protestants. In particular, in the second half of the nineteenth century the city of Belfast rose to rival Dublin in size and outweigh it in economic importance because of its growing shipbuilding industry. Belfast was a majority Protestant city and the Home Rule issue in 1886 led to riots as Protestants of all classes took to the streets to reject the idea of being ruled by an all-Ireland Home Rule Parliament in which Roman Catholics would be the majority. From this point on the position of Ulster was a key factor in the overall Irish Question.

- Between 1880 and 1891 Irish politics was dominated by Charles Stewart Parnell who emerged as a great nationalist leader, despite his being an Anglican landowner. Parnell raised the Irish National Party to the point where it held the balance of power in the House of Commons and seriously influenced the two major parties. However, Parnell was a controversial figure and his involvement with a married woman ending in a scandalous divorce case split the party into two groups and left it in a bitter state of recrimination. In 1891, before the dispute could be resolved, Parnell died leaving his supporters and opponents still at odds with each other. In 1895 therefore many Irishmen had lost interest in politics. The land question seemed to have been largely resolved. The Irish National Party seemed to be a waste of time as it appeared more interested in its internal division than in representing Ireland at Westminster.

The British Perspective

From the point of view of the mainstream British politicians at the end of the nineteenth century, Ireland could never be allowed to be politically independent from Great Britain for the following reasons:

Key question
Why was Great Britain so determined to resist Irish independence?

- Too many influential people in Great Britain owned land or held business interests in Ireland. Most of these people were opposed even to allowing Home Rule for Ireland, let alone accepting its complete separation. Indeed, even supporters of Home Rule, such as Gladstone, argued in its favour on the basis that it would satisfy moderate Irish opinion and end any widespread demand for independence.

Figure 6.1: Map showing Ireland in relation to the British mainland and continental Europe.

- Economically, Ireland was seen as integral to the economy of the British Isles as a whole and thus could not be allowed to go its own way without disruption to the British economy. Again, Home Rule would not have allowed economic independence.

- In imperial terms the independence of Ireland would have had (it was argued) disastrous effects on the unity of the Empire as a whole. How could the Empire be expected to remain intact if the United Kingdom itself could not do so?

- Most important of all was the strategic issue. Ireland lay on the other side of the British mainland from continental Europe (see Figure 6.1, page 109). Great Britain could not afford to allow Irish independence as this might have compromised security in the event of a war with a major continental power. Suppose Ireland decided to side with the continental power or was invaded and overrun? In those circumstances Britain would face the disruption of sea access to British ports from the Atlantic and the possibility of invasion from two sides. From a strategic point of view Ireland's independence was out of the question.

When the second Home Rule Bill was defeated by an overwhelming majority in the House of Lords in 1893, Gladstone was keen to fight another general election on the issue. He hoped to get a firm overall liberal majority that could force the Lords to accept Home Rule. His colleagues in the Cabinet, however, were not prepared to support this course of action. They believed, almost certainly correctly, that there was no real support for the policy in the country at large. Gladstone therefore resigned and was replaced by Lord Rosebery, who then shelved Home Rule for an unspecified period.

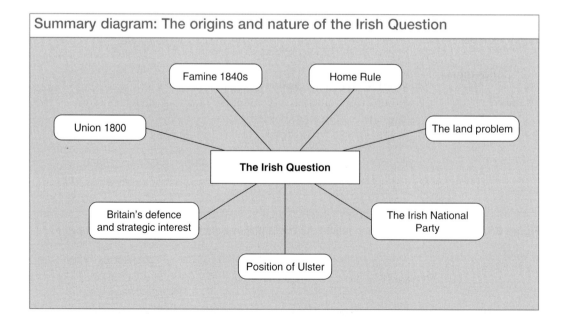

Summary diagram: The origins and nature of the Irish Question

Famine 1840s

Home Rule

Union 1800

The land problem

The Irish Question

Britain's defence and strategic interest

The Irish National Party

Position of Ulster

2 | 1895–1909: The Revival of Political Nationalism

In these circumstances, it might be considered surprising that Ireland entered a relatively peaceful period between 1893 and the introduction of the third Home Rule Bill in 1912. Political apathy ruled the day. Many Irishmen had not really expected Home Rule to pass anyway and the improvement in the general condition of Ireland meant that many Irishmen felt that Home Rule was not that vital and could be left until political conditions meant there was better chance of success. After all, the Liberals were still committed to the policy in principle. However, this did not mean that Irish nationalism was now a thing of the past.

A cultural revival

National pride and aspirations found their expression, increasingly, in a great cultural revival that emphasised the importance of restoring the status of the Irish language, which had long been in decline. Irish sports began to flourish; Irish literature, dance and music recruited new enthusiasts. This movement was marked by the formation of organisations such as the Gaelic League, founded in 1893, and by the expansion of earlier groups such as the Gaelic Athletic Association (1884). Even so, despite the unthreatening tone of the cultural revival, nationalism of this kind could not be wholly divorced from a political context.

The fundamental message of the revival was anti-British. It condemned what was often called '**West Britonism**' and encouraged a separate Irish consciousness. It required only a change in the political climate to harness this sense of a separate Irish identity to a new and specifically Irish political agenda.

The government's position 1895–1909

The alliance of Conservatives and Liberal Unionists, which formed the Unionist Government of 1895–1905, hoped to bury the issue of Home Rule once and for all. The Land Act of 1903, usually known as 'Wyndham's Act' after George Wyndham, the Chief Secretary for Ireland, substantially completed the transfer of land from landlords to tenants. This was the cornerstone of the Unionist strategy by which Ireland was to be pacified.

The Irish National Party was in two minds about this process. On the one hand, they could hardly condemn the end of the hated '**landlordism**'; on the other, they recognised that with its passing they had lost one of their most potent political weapons. They consoled themselves with the thought that the Liberal Party remained pledged to the introduction of Home Rule and waited on events.

In 1906 this policy of patience appeared to have paid off when the Liberals won a great victory in the general election. The Liberals now had so great a parliamentary majority that they could, if necessary, contemplate a constitutional clash with the House of Lords if the peers proved obstructive to measures

Key question
How did Irish nationalism manifest itself in the period before 1914?

Key date
Third Home Rule Bill introduced: 1912

Key terms
West Britonism
The idea that Ireland had no real separate identity but was merely a geographical area of Britain.

Landlordism
System of land use where real power resides with those who own the land at the expense of those who actually work on it.

Key question
How did the British Government try to resolve the Irish Question between 1895 and 1909?

passed with massive support in the Commons. This was the situation Gladstone had dreamed of, but could never achieve. Unfortunately for the Irish Party, his successors had inherited his pledge but not his commitment. From the outset the Liberal Government was determined not to allow Irish affairs to dominate their administration.

Although the policy of Home Rule was not abandoned, it was no longer to be the primary objective as Gladstone had desired. The Liberals between 1906 and 1909 preferred to embark upon a general policy of social reform, before considering any fundamental constitutional change. The Prime Minister, Campbell-Bannerman, and his successor, Asquith, both feared that Home Rule would provoke a constitutional crisis that might result in the loss of their majority at a general election. They were therefore determined to secure social reform first. This was an exact reversal of Gladstone's priorities.

Nor was there much that the Irish Party could do to force the issue. The Government was not dependent on Irish support and was aware that Home Rule had never aroused much support or even interest among the English electorate, to whom social and economic issues were of far more importance.

The emergence of the 'New Nationalists'

In the meantime, in Ireland itself, new nationalist forces were taking shape that would ultimately control Irish destinies and destroy the Irish National Party.

Key question
Why had Irish nationalism become stronger by 1906?

James Connolly

A **labour movement** was growing, under the control of James Connolly, an ardent socialist and trade union organiser.

Connolly was motivated by the Marxist belief that socialism could be achieved only when a country was sufficiently industrialised for the industrial workers (or proletariat) to be strong enough to overthrow 'capitalist oppression'. He believed that Ireland had remained largely agricultural because it was forced to serve the wider needs of the British economy. To Connolly, Irish independence was essential if Ireland was ever to reach the stage at which a socialist state could be established.

In aiming for a **Socialist Workers' Republic**, and in linking that idea with trade unionism, Connolly made a major breakthrough in the cause of Irish nationalism. He won over the urban working classes in Dublin to republicanism and therefore, by definition, to **separatism**. This provided a new and important political driving force for independence from Britain.

Sinn Fein

Connolly's movement, with its newspaper, the *Workers' Republic*, and its group of activists – the Citizen Army – was opposed by another new nationalist force, Sinn Fein (meaning 'ourselves alone'), founded by Arthur Griffith in 1905. This movement, through its paper *The United Irishmen*, rejected Connolly's ideas of

Labour movement
Principle of organising the working classes so that they can achieve better conditions.

Socialist Workers' Republic
Political system where government is based on the principle of a socialist state controlled by the working classes.

Separatism
Principle of separating Ireland from Great Britain.

Key terms

socialism and violent revolution as well as the Irish National Party's constitutional approach.

Instead, Griffith wanted a system of peaceful resistance in which a voluntary parliament would be formed to govern Ireland in defiance of the British Government. In effect this meant simply carrying on as if Ireland was already independent and ignoring British institutions, such as the courts and civil administration, as though they did not exist.

The essence of Griffith's policy was a kind of federal solution, in which Ireland and Great Britain would have been made more equal in status. A similar system had been used by Austria and Hungary in the 1860s and had successfully improved their relations within the Austrian Empire. For this reason Griffith's plan was sometimes referred to by contemporaries as 'The Austrian Solution'.

Griffith did not want a republic and he did not want the overthrow of capitalism. He aimed to create conditions in which capitalism could flourish more to the benefit of the Irish people.

Underground groups

Apart from these two open organisations, there remained the underground groups dedicated to the **Fenian** tradition, such as the Irish Republican Brotherhood (IRB). Though republican, the IRB had no clearly defined political philosophy: it was not Marxist, and it therefore had little natural sympathy with Connolly's movement. Its commitment to violence repelled Griffith.

Thus there were serious areas of division between the various strands of Irish nationalism and, in these circumstances, the Irish National Party faced little in the way of a serious challenge to its continued domination of Irish politics.

3 | The Impact of the Constitutional Crisis 1909–11

In 1909 the British political scene began to change dramatically. The crisis over the 1909 Budget (see pages 68–70) resulted in some momentous developments for Ireland. The general election at the beginning of 1910 saw the Liberals lose their overall majority in the House of Commons. From now on they were to be a minority government, with the Irish Nationalist MPs holding the balance of power. This was followed by a constitutional crisis that ended with the passing of the Parliament Act of 1911 (see pages 72–4), which deprived the House of Lords of its indefinite veto over legislation.

These changes put Irish Home Rule right back at the top of the political agenda again. During the budget crisis, John Redmond, the Irish National Party leader, had opposed a proposal to increase whiskey duties on the grounds that it would adversely affect Irish distilleries. In the crisis over the Parliament Act he based his support for the government on the assurance that Irish Home Rule would be a priority once the curbing of the powers of the House of Lords had been achieved. In his

Key term

Fenian
Late-nineteenth-century group of Irish Nationalists whose aim was Irish independence. They organised a rising in 1827 and carried out bombings in British cities. They recruited heavily in the USA from Irish immigrants.

Key question
How did events in British politics affect the cause of Irish Nationalism?

Key dates

Irish National Party holds balance of power in the House of Commons as result of the general election: 1910

Parliament Act removes the power of the House of Lords to permanently stand in the way of Home Rule: 1911

negotiations with the Liberals he had made it clear that the Irish would act to disrupt government policy if Home Rule remained on the shelf.

The Liberals' position

Redmond's threat of disruption was in many ways a bluff since there was no alternative government from which he could expect to obtain Home Rule. It was however a bluff that was not called. The Liberal commitment to Home Rule, though not as passionate as Gladstone's had been, was nevertheless genuine. This was not to say, however, that the Irish Party could simply present its demands and expect them to be met in full. Asquith, the Prime Minister, intended to introduce a limited Home Rule Bill that could not be credibly represented by Unionists as paving the way for eventual independence. This was unrealistic as a strategy because the Unionists were bound to argue, and with some justification, that any measure of 'Home Rule' was bound to stimulate further nationalist demands.

Other leading Liberals, like Lloyd George and Winston Churchill, believed that a separate deal for the largely Protestant and pro-British Ulster counties would have to be devised in the end. Asquith knew they would face fanatical opposition within Ulster itself, along with strong resistance from the Unionist Party in Britain.

The Parliament Act, which was the key to overcoming opposition in the House of Lords, was in reality something of a mixed blessing. It ensured that a Home Rule Bill could be passed, but since the peers could reject the Bill twice before being constitutionally compelled to accept it on the third occasion, it also meant that there would be a minimum period of two years before enactment, during which opponents could take up extreme positions.

4 | The Third Home Rule Bill 1912

Key question
Why was the Third Home Rule Bill a contentious issue?

The Third Home Rule Bill was introduced into the House of Commons in April 1912. The terms were:

- An Irish Parliament with an elected House of Commons and a nominated upper chamber called the Senate with limited powers, especially restricted in financial affairs.
- Forty-two Irish MPs still to sit at Westminster.
- Ulster was to be included in the new Home Rule Parliament.

It was a moderate proposal leaving considerable control of Irish affairs with the Westminster Parliament. It constituted a limited devolution of self-government.

- To Redmond it was barely acceptable and could only be sold to the more extreme INP members as a starting-point for future progress.
- To the Unionists it was entirely unacceptable for the same reason and because of the inclusion of Ulster.

Bonar Law, the Unionist leader, was provoked into an extreme stance when, in July 1912, at a huge Unionist rally at Blenheim Palace, he observed that he could 'imagine no length of resistance to which Ulster can go, in which I should not be prepared to support them'. Asquith responded by calling Bonar Law's speech 'reckless' and 'a complete grammar of anarchy'.

In this bitter atmosphere the Bill passed the Commons for the first time, eventually completing its stormy passage in January 1913. There was great disorder in the House during the debates and verbal abuse was common. The verdict of the Commons was immediately reversed in the Lords. The whole process then had to be repeated, with totally predictable results.

By August 1913 the Bill had passed once more through the Commons, only to receive its routine rejection by the peers. A proposal for a constitutional conference in September 1913 foundered on the uncompromising positions taken by the opposing forces. The most that the Ulster leader, Sir Edward Carson, would accept was Home Rule excluding the whole of the nine counties of Ulster Province. These included the counties of Cavan, Donegal and Monaghan – all of which had Roman Catholic majority populations. These were impossible terms for Redmond and the most that Asquith would concede was a limited degree of independence for Ulster, within the Home Rule provisions. The scene was set for a new constitutional crisis.

The Unionist resistance

While attention had been focused on the fate of the Home Rule Bill at Westminster, events had been moving in Ireland itself. Ulster opinion had been hardening into die-hard resistance well before the introduction of the Bill and, in Sir Edward Carson, it had found an able and articulate leader.

In September 1912, Carson drew up a 'Solemn League and Covenant' whose signatories pledged themselves to resist a Home Rule Parliament in Ireland should one ever be set up. Over 470,000 people signed this covenant – some of the more passionate using their own blood as ink.

In January 1913 the Ulster Volunteer Force was set up and soon numbered 100,000 men. This provoked the setting up of a nationalist counterpart organisation, the Irish National Volunteers, a body pledged to support Redmond, but which was quickly infiltrated by the Irish Republican Brotherhood. The creation of two groups with totally opposed objectives meant that the long-feared risk of civil war began to emerge as a real possibility.

In December 1913, Asquith's government resorted to a ban, by Royal Proclamation, on the importation of arms and ammunition into Ireland. Neither of the two paramilitary forces was as yet properly armed, and the precaution seemed wise. At the same time Asquith was also preparing to extract more concessions from the Irish National Party, in the hope that the opposition in Parliament to Home Rule could at least be reduced. This could only be done by putting pressure on Redmond.

Key question
In what ways did the Ulster Crisis affect the Home Rule controversy?

Key date
The Ulster Crisis – Ireland on brink of civil war over issue of Home Rule: 1912–13

He was persuaded, with great difficulty, to accept the exclusion of Ulster from Home Rule for a temporary period – initially set at three years, but almost immediately doubled to six. The concession compromised the whole concept of Ireland as a single unit and can be seen as the first clear move towards the idea of **partition**, but in reality it was a risk Redmond felt he could take, because it seemed unlikely that Carson would ever accept any temporary exclusion. Carson duly obliged by rejecting the proposal as soon as Asquith put it forward.

Partition
The separation of a single area into two or more distinct areas under separate authority.

Key term

The Curragh Mutiny

In March 1914 the so-called 'Curragh Mutiny' rocked the government. The government had long been concerned that, in the event of a confrontation with the Ulster Unionists, the enforcement of Home Rule would depend on the Army.

The Army units in Ireland were largely controlled by officers of an Anglo-Irish Protestant background who were overwhelmingly Unionist in their sentiments. In an attempt to lessen the risk of widespread resignations from the army in protest against Home Rule, the Secretary of State for War, Jack Seely, approved instructions to General Sir Arthur Paget, the Commander-in-Chief in Ireland, that officers whose homes were actually in Ulster could be allowed a temporary leave from duty. There were rumours that the government was about to order the arrest of the Ulster leaders (they had been considering this for some time), and Paget, in briefing his officers, was deliberately pessimistic, suggesting that Ulster would be 'in a blaze by Saturday'.

As a result, 58 officers, including a Brigadier-General, resigned. Action against the defectors was impossible because sympathy for them was widespread throughout the army. The government was forced to conciliate the rebels and Seely even went so far as to suggest that force would not be used against the opponents of Home Rule.

Although Seely was obliged to resign, the government appeared weak and indecisive. The Ulster Volunteers were encouraged to take action to arm themselves. In April, a series of landings of armaments took place along the Ulster coast. There was no interference from the authorities and the Ulster Volunteers were suddenly transformed into a well-armed and formidable army.

It was only a matter of time before the Irish National Volunteers responded. In June, guns for the Nationalists were landed near Dublin, but this time the authorities intervened – leading to three people dead and nearly 40 injured. Although it was by no means as successful an effort as the Ulster landings, it still left considerable quantities of arms in the hands of the nationalist force.

Attempts at compromise

Meanwhile, the Home Rule Bill was heading for its final passage. Asquith, Bonar Law and Carson had agreed by June that an additional Amending Bill would be introduced and include some

Key question
How did the Liberal Government attempt to resolve the crisis?

form of compromise. This in itself was of little use, however, since there was no agreement as to what these amendments should be. Furthermore, any amendments would either have to be accepted by or imposed on Redmond and the Irish National Party.

In late June, the government produced its first attempt at an amending bill. The main proposal was for the exclusion of the Ulster counties from the Home Rule Bill for a period of six years, with each county voting separately for its future. This idea had already been rejected by Carson and the House of Lords amended the proposal to provide for the automatic exclusion of all nine Ulster counties on a permanent basis. This solution the government could not accept.

Encouraged by King George V, the politicians convened a constitutional conference at Buckingham Palace on 21 July 1914:

• Asquith and Lloyd George represented the government
• Redmond and John Dillon the INP
• Bonar Law and Lord Lansdowne the Unionist Party
• Carson and James Craig the Ulster Unionists.

The conference was intended to reach decisions in two stages:

• First to debate the area of Ulster to be excluded.
• Second to debate the terms of exclusion, whether they were to be temporary or permanent, and, if the former, then for how long.

In the event the discussions broke down at the first stage and so the second stage was never even considered. After three days of deadlock, the conference was abandoned. Barely a week later, the European crisis came to a head and Britain was at war with Germany.

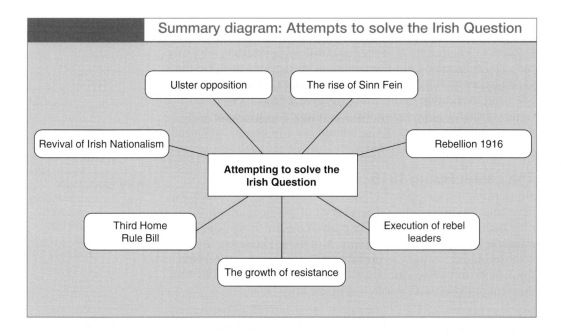

Summary diagram: Attempts to solve the Irish Question

Ulster opposition

The rise of Sinn Fein

Revival of Irish Nationalism

Rebellion 1916

Attempting to solve the Irish Question

Third Home Rule Bill

Execution of rebel leaders

The growth of resistance

5 | The Impact of First World War 1914–18

The crisis of war overtook the Irish Question at a crucial point. All sides in the constitutional conference realised that some kind of compromise was inevitable. Carson, in particular, was far more moderate in private than he was prepared to be in public. If the parties had been forced to continue the negotiations, a constitutional settlement would almost certainly have been reached.

In the event, the war enabled all sides to agree to shelve the issue in a way that virtually guaranteed the renewal of the crisis at some later date. The Home Rule Act was passed as an all-Ireland measure but was accompanied by a Suspensory Order, which made it inoperable for the duration of the war. This was just about the worst outcome, short of actual civil war, that could possibly have been contrived for the Ulster Crisis.

Initially, the First World War seemed to have a positive effect upon Anglo-Irish relations. Support for the war was almost universal at the outset, with the fate of 'little Belgium' seeming to represent the interests of all small nations in their relations with those greater than themselves. In comparison to the threat of German militarism, even British rule seemed benign (see Chapter 7).

Ulster, already intoxicated with 'loyalism' to the British Crown, rushed to the colours in a frenzy of patriotism. In the rest of Ireland the response was less passionate but nevertheless the men of Catholic Ireland also answered the call and marched to slaughter in France and Belgium. Probably never before in her history had Ireland seemed to be so much in harmony with Britain.

For John Redmond the war seemed the ideal opportunity for nationalist Ireland to demonstrate her loyalty to the Crown and secure, by her war effort, the future of Ireland under Home Rule. Even before the war he had, for political reasons, taken control over the running of the Irish National Volunteers. Now he used his authority to bring them into the war. First he declared that the Volunteers would defend Ireland against invasion, thus releasing the regular army to fight the Germans in the front line. He then went further and urged them to fight overseas. This move was intended to reassure opinion in England of Irish loyalty, but to go so far was dangerous. Redmond was tolerated rather than respected by the leaders of the Volunteers and he was no Parnell in terms of his popular appeal.

The Easter Rising 1916

Support for the war split the National Volunteers. The majority, reflecting the overwhelming sentiment of public opinion, sided with Redmond and followed the path of loyalty to the Empire by enlisting to fight against Germany. A minority, however, broke with Redmond, seeing the pro-war stance as collaboration with the British and a betrayal of Ireland's claim to nationhood. This drew them closer to Connolly's 'Citizen Army'.

Key question
In what ways did the outbreak of war in 1914 present both opportunities and dangers for the relationship between Great Britain and Ireland?

Key question
Was the Easter Rising a miscalculation on the part of the Irish Republicans?

Key date

Easter Rising – Irish Independence proclaimed but rebels defeated and leaders executed: 1918

Origins of the Rising

Herein lay the origin of the Easter Rising of 1916. To extreme nationalists the danger Britain faced in Europe was an opportunity to strike for freedom and set up an Irish Republic. A small group planned the Rising, including:

- Tom Clarke, a shopkeeper and former Fenian who had spent 15 years in prison for bombing offences
- Patrick Pearse, a teacher
- James Connolly, the trade union leader and head of the Citizen Army.

Pearse in particular was deeply committed to the idea that Ireland's future could be redeemed only by a 'blood sacrifice'. In other words, even if the intended revolution failed, it would have purged the soul of Ireland that had been compromised by years of collaboration with the British oppressors.

The outcome of the Rising

The rebellion was ill-timed, ill-planned and chaotically carried out. Many of these failings were not entirely the fault of the revolutionary leaders themselves:

- They were obliged to keep their plans secret, even from some of the key personnel involved, in order to maintain security.
- They counted on support from Germany in the form of an arms shipment, which was intercepted and so never arrived.
- The Commanding Officer of the National Volunteers, Eoin McNeill, was not informed of the plans until the last possible moment because the plotters were not sure how he would react. Initially he reluctantly gave his support, but when he learned that the arms shipment had been lost he did everything he could to stop the *coup* attempt. He cancelled the Volunteers' planned marches for Easter Sunday, which were supposed to be the starting point for the Rising. The rebel leaders were forced to improvise by rescheduling the marches and the rising for Easter Monday.

Militarily the Easter Rising was doomed to fail from the start. The number of rebels mobilised was far too few and they were inadequately armed. The declaration of Irish Independence and an Irish Republic was read by Patrick Pearse to a small, bewildered crowd, outside the General Post Office in Dublin, the headquarters of the Rebellion. The rebels successfully took over several key strategic points of access to the city, but had insufficient numbers to do more than wait for the reaction of the British Government. Even if the attempt had attracted immediate and widespread popular support, which it did not, the odds would have been against the rebels.

Reaction to the Rising

Key question
What were the immediate effects of the Rising?

In the event, the Rising flew in the face of popular feeling and was almost universally condemned by the Irish people. Nevertheless, the rebels held the British Army at bay for the best

The wreck of a burnt out car in front of bombed buildings forms a barricade during the Easter Rising, Dublin, 1916.

part of a week and, although many saw no actual fighting at all before surrendering, some fought with great skill and courage against overwhelming odds before they were killed or captured.

The centre of Dublin was reduced to rubble by British artillery fire. Fires raged out of control and the city took on the look of one of the war zones of the western front. This was glorious defeat when compared to the fiasco of the Fenian Rising of 1867, and its potential for exploitation by the extremists was immediately apparent to the Irish National Party, who urged leniency for the captured rebels upon the British Government.

These pleas fell on largely deaf ears. Admittedly, of over 70 death sentences initially passed, the great majority were changed to terms of imprisonment, but any executions were likely to be controversial, given the nature of Irish history. In the end, 14 of the leaders, including Pearse and Connolly, were shot and one further execution took place of a rebel who had killed a policeman while resisting arrest. As the executions progressed, so the mood in Ireland began to change and the fears of the Irish MPs grew.

The aftermath of the Easter Rising 1916–18

The policy of executions brought about a most profound change in the atmosphere in Ireland. Few ordinary people knew much about the revolutionary leaders (apart perhaps from James Connolly) or their aims. The Rising became popularly known as the 'Sinn Fein' Rebellion, although, in fact, Sinn Fein had no involvement in it.

Gradually, however, the leaders and those they had led were transformed into heroic figures. When the captured groups of rebels had been marched to the Dublin docks to be shipped off to prison on the mainland, they had needed army protection from angry mobs of mothers, fathers, wives, sisters and even children

Key question
How and why did the mood in Catholic Ireland change from one of support for Britain to support for Sinn Fein?

The rebels in the Easter Rising – James Connolly (left) and
Patrick Pearse (right).

of Irish soldiers fighting in France and Belgium, who had tried to
attack them as cowards and traitors. Now these same people, for
the most part, were demanding their release. The government
was in too difficult a position, at a crucial stage in the war, to
adopt a lenient policy towards those who had committed treason.
Nevertheless, it is impossible to escape the conclusion that, had
the executions not been carried out, the subsequent course of
Irish history might have been very different.

The rebellion and its aftermath polarised attitudes in Ireland
even further:

- In Protestant unionist opinion, the rebels were traitors who had
  got what they deserved.
- In Catholic nationalist opinion, they were heroes and martyrs.

British government's actions 1917–18

Key question
Did the British
Government
mismanage its
handling of the Easter
Rebellion and Ireland
during the rest of the
Great War?

From this point onwards, the prospect of achieving an all-Ireland
settlement by consensus was virtually extinguished. In 1917,
Asquith, alarmed that the Irish Question might sour relations
with the then still neutral United States, offered immediate Home
Rule with a provision for the exclusion of the six north-eastern
counties of Ulster where there was a substantial Protestant
majority. The government also sponsored a convention to discuss
the long-term future of the six counties. These initiatives had no
chance of success. The Sinn Fein Party, which was now an alliance
of Griffith's original organisation and the remnants of the 1916
rebels, refused even to attend the convention.

At the end of 1917, the remainder of the rebels interned on the
mainland were released as a goodwill gesture. But, though
welcomed in Ireland, this did little to improve the image of the
British Government. In 1918 it put the seal on the failure of its

Irish Policy by extending conscription to Ireland. Even the Irish National Party opposed this move, but its show of resistance to British authority came too late to save it from the backlash of public opinion in nationalist Ireland, now moving firmly in support of Sinn Fein.

The 1918 general election marked the end for the Irish National Party. It was decimated as a political force, winning only seven seats against the triumphant 73 won by Sinn Fein. Even allowing for some vote rigging by Sinn Fein, there is little doubt that the result reflected a genuine demand in Ireland for a substantial degree of independence from Britain. The elected Sinn Fein candidates refused to take their places at Westminster, preferring instead to set up 'Dail Eireann' – the Assembly of Ireland – claiming to represent the only legitimate legislative authority for the country.

Over the next three years the situation in Ireland would deteriorate into a bloody guerrilla war of assassinations and brutality by both sides. In 1921 a compromise agreement would leave Ireland partitioned into North and South. The North was to remain as part of the United Kingdom, while the South became initially a self-governing Dominion of the British Empire and eventually the Irish Republic. This strategy would, by its failure, result in further death and misery for the rest of the century.

> **Key date**
>
> Sinn Fein Nationalist Party wins majority of Irish seats and declares Ireland independent from Great Britain: 1918

Study Guide: AS Questions

In the style of AQA

Examine the extent to which the First World War was a key turning point in the development Irish Nationalism in the period 1895–1921.

Study tips

The cross-references are intended to take you straight to the material that will help you to answer the question.

The approach is as for all evaluative essay questions. You must fully consider the case for arguing that the First World War was a key turning point – in this case there is compelling evidence to support that conclusion (page 118). However, take each case on its merits – other titles might well pose a position that is less easy to defend, so be open minded in your approach. To obtain high marks you must be balanced in your discussion and reach a clear judgement. Start by focusing on how the First World War may have been a key turning point in the development of Irish Nationalism then balance this against a range of possible alternative explanations/interpretations in your answer.

- For example, you might argue that it was not the war itself that was the turning point but the Irish Rebellion, which might well have occurred even had the war not been in progress (pages 118–21).
- Another possibility is the 1906 general election that returned the Liberal Government, committed to Home Rule (pages 111–12).

- The general election of 1910 that left the Liberals dependent on the INP in the House of Commons deserves consideration (pages 71–2), as does the failure to secure the Home Rule Bill during the Ulster Crisis (pages 114–15).

Credit is given for evidence of a more probing analysis, so in this case you ought to consider the fact that 'Irish Nationalism' is a term that covers a number of different groups and aims; for example, the extremists and the moderates need to be differentiated.

In the style of Edexcel

Why did the Liberal Government try, and fail, to give Home Rule to Ireland in the years 1910–14?   (15 marks)

Source: Edexcel, January 2003

Exam tips

The cross-references are intended to take you straight to the material that will help you to answer the question.

As with all Unit 2 causation questions for Edexcel you must do more than simply list reasons. The more you can do to analyse the material the higher your mark will go. It is vital to discuss the relative importance of the factors that influenced the Liberal Government and equally important to establish links and the interaction between them wherever possible. Here the best approach is to classify the causal factors into two categories:

- Those that represent the willingness of the Liberals to proceed with Home Rule (page 114).
- Those that constrained them to introduce the third Home Rule Bill in 1912 (pages 114–17).

It is therefore necessary to show that the Liberals were committed to the principle of Home Rule long before 1912 and that in introducing the Bill they were therefore only carrying out what had long been the official policy of the Party.

It is also fair to point out that many, though not all, Liberals genuinely believed that Home Rule was the best solution for Ireland. However, the fact remains that the Liberals did not introduce Home Rule in the period after 1906 when they had a massive majority – they only introduced it in 1912 following the constitutional crisis when they had lost their overall majority. You therefore need to discuss:

- their dependence on the INP in the House of Commons (pages 71–2)
- the effect of the Parliament Act of 1911, which deprived the House of Lords of its power of veto and made it for the first time possible to pass Home Rule even in the face of Lords' opposition (pages 113–14).

In the style of OCR

Assess the consequences of the Irish problem from 1909 to 1916.

Source: OCR, June 2003

Exam tips

The cross-references are intended to take you straight to the material that will help you to answer the question.

With questions like this always look at the dates: is there anything about 1909 that stands out, i.e. the onset of the constitutional crisis that was going to accentuate the importance of the position of the INP (pages 71–2)? The year 1916 should draw your attention to the Easter Rising (pages 118–21).

It is no good simply going through what happened. You must try to relate events in Ireland to consequences for the Liberals and Conservatives in Britain, i.e. how they were affected by the situation in Ireland. For example:

- The constitutional crisis itself was intensified by the Lords' realisation that, if they gave way on the Parliament Bill, this would affect their ability to resist Home Rule in the future – arguably had it not been for that consideration the crisis might have been resolved earlier and with less hostility (page 114).
- Explain and discuss the Ulster Crisis – it did after all have a massively distracting effect on the government in the summer of 1914 and, arguably, was a factor in their belated and confused response to the European crisis that was developing (page 118).

When you are assessing the factors you need to evaluate their relative significance in changing the course of events and draw out how they are linked and interrelated.

7 Reform, Confrontation and Total War

POINTS TO CONSIDER
The First World War had a major impact on Britain. By its end so much had changed that many people felt that Britain was almost unrecognisable as the country that had entered the war in 1914. This chapter will examine the impact of the war through the following themes:

- British politics on the eve of the First World War
- The decline of the Liberal Party – was it doomed before the start of the war?
- British foreign policy and the outbreak of war in 1914
- The political impact of the war
- Women and the war
- The social and economic impact of the war.

Key dates

1914	Britain declares war on Germany and her allies
1915	Coalition government formed of Liberals, Conservatives and Labour
1916	Lloyd George forms a new coalition government
	The Liberal Party splits and Asquith goes into opposition
1918	Act to enfranchise all men over 21 and most women over 30
	Victory over Germany

1 | British Politics on the Eve of the First World War

Key question
How genuinely opposed to each other were the Conservatives and Liberals in this period?

Much of the period covered in this book has been concerned with confrontations of one kind or another: Ireland; votes for women; democracy versus privilege; free trade versus protectionism.

In particular, the relationship between Liberalism and Unionism seems to have been one of unremitting hostility over a period of years:

- The issue of tariff reform raised by Joseph Chamberlain and its eventual acceptance by the Unionist Party seemed to polarise party principles into the opposite corners of free trade and protectionism.
- The constitutional crisis confirmed that division and led into the bitter period of confrontation surrounding the Ulster crisis of 1912–14 (see pages 114–17).

On the eve of the First World War, therefore, it would seem at first sight that the two main political parties had never been further apart in their policies and rarely more hostile in their attitude to each other.

The bitter political climate worried many contemporaries who saw in it the seeds of the disintegration of the political system. Few could have predicted that a war would soon engulf Europe and, temporarily at least, make the divisions that had previously emerged irrelevant.

Political consensus?

Lloyd George's proposal for a coalition government (see page 73), dismissed as impractical in 1910, became a reality in 1915 under the pressure of war. Coalitions were to rule the country for 21 out of the next 30 years. Of course, the circumstances that brought these coalitions about and then kept them together were exceptional, but the ease with which politicians of all parties accepted them reveals something deeper about the nature of politics in the period before the First World War.

Britain declares war on Germany and her allies: 1914

Coalition government formed of Liberals, Conservatives and Labour: 1915

Key dates

The reality was that, underneath the apparent hostility, there was a greater degree of consensus than the confrontational atmosphere would suggest. This was particularly true of the leaders of the parties. Their public clashes seemed to be the essence of the highly charged political atmosphere. Yet, all the time, behind the scenes, these same leaders were to be found seeking compromises and conciliations which were often wrecked, not by their mutual hostilities, but by the nature of the problems they were seeking to resolve.

For example, during the constitutional crisis, the failure to reach a compromise was largely due to the fact that neither side could afford, politically, to be seen to be giving in, rather than to the existence of a genuinely unbridgeable gulf. During the Ulster crisis it was the entrenched positions of the Irish Nationalist and Ulster Unionist leaders, rather than those of Asquith and Bonar Law, which made progress in the 1914 negotiations impossible (see page 117).

On a broad range of issues there was a remarkable degree of consensus among the major politicians on both sides on the following issues.

Social reform

The Unionists were more willing to consider social reform than is often supposed and, after 1903, free traders and tariff reformers within the Unionist Party sought to outbid each other with promises of reform. Once the economy went into a slump between 1907 and 1910 the Unionists, by now committed to some kind of new deal on tariffs, linked their policy to social reform and tried to compete with the Liberals on the issue. The desire to preserve values of individual responsibility in social policy was, if anything, stronger among the more traditional Liberals than it was among the Unionists.

Female suffrage

The demand for female suffrage found both supporters and opponents among the Liberals and Unionists and both sides were ultimately more concerned about the practical political problems that the issue posed than they were about the moral principle.

Free trade versus protectionism

Even the division between Liberalism and Unionism over protection was not as clear-cut as it appeared. The support of the Liberal leaders for free trade was a political necessity. Privately, leaders such as Asquith and Lloyd George knew that there was a case to be made for the reform of fiscal policy: specifically, the means of obtaining government revenue.

The Budget of 1909 was barely sufficient to meet the projected spending requirements of immediate policies. Even with Lloyd George's unprecedented tax increases, the government still required a £3 million transfer from the **sinking fund** in order to balance the books. It was obvious that some other method of raising revenue would be needed in the longer term if further social reform were to be contemplated.

Key term

Sinking fund
A government fund into which money is put for paying off government debts as they become due for repayment.

Internal divisions

The picture that emerges of political life in the period before the First World War is one in which the two main parties were as divided internally as they were from each other. This is especially true of the relationships between the party leaders and their respective followers.

Both Liberal and Unionist leaders had to face the problem of trying to reconcile conflicting attitudes within their parliamentary parties and in the constituencies at large. Frequently it was not simply a case of trying to accommodate differing opinions, but also of trying to force party members to abandon their prejudices and face up to political realities. It is hardly surprising in these circumstances that the party leaders frequently found it easier to deal with each other, than to satisfy the demands of their own supporters.

Key question
Was the Liberal Party doomed to decline in 1914?

2 | The Decline of the Liberal Party

In 1936, at a point where the fortunes of the Liberal Party had sunk low and its future existence was a matter in some doubt, G.R. Dangerfield, in what became a famous book, *The Strange Death of Liberal England*, put forward an explanation for the decline of the once great party. According to Dangerfield, the crucial period in the Liberal decline was 1911–14, following the constitutional crisis, during which basic inadequacies and limitations of liberalism had made the government incapable of governing effectively.

This view did not gain universal acceptance in the years that followed. The general trend in studies of the Liberal Party was to look for alternative explanations for the Party's decline. A particular view emerged that Liberal decline had set in much earlier than Dangerfield supposed – the idea that it might not have been in decline before 1914 was not seriously considered.

The topic became more controversial however with the appearance in 1966 of Trevor Wilson's book *The Downfall of the Liberal Party*, which argued that the decline of the Liberal Party was the result of the damaging split that developed during the First World War between Asquith and Lloyd George (see page 136). According to this view the Liberal Party remained an effective political force in 1914 and could have gone on indefinitely as a major party competing with the Conservatives for power.

Until the publication of Wilson's book, the decline of the Liberal Party had received little attention from Labour historians since it had been assumed that the fall of the Party could be satisfactorily explained by the Dangerfield thesis or the various alternatives and, more importantly, as the natural result of the rise of the Labour Party.

The impact of the First World War

The impact of the First World War had been regarded as simply the accelerator of a natural process of political evolution. The Labour Party, as the fittest instrument for advancing social reform and representing working-class aspirations, had inherited the role of opposition to the forces of conservatism.

Following the publication of the 'Wilson thesis', a number of other historians began to develop the argument that the Liberal Party had still had a bright future in British politics on the eve of the war. These historians, for the most part, concentrated on the impact of 'New Liberalism' in order to argue that the party had freed itself of the limitations that had been imposed on it by Gladstonian principles, and had become a party with a relevant message and electoral appeal in an increasingly democratic and class-based political climate. The clear implication of this view was that the Labour Party was destined either to remain a minor third force on the political fringe or to be absorbed into the Liberal Party. Such a concept naturally incensed those Labour historians for whom the rise of the Labour Party was a matter of unquestionable destiny.

A series of studies intended to counter Wilson's arguments came to a conclusion in 1974, in the publication of Ross McKibbin's book, *The Evolution of the Labour Party 1910–1924*, which emphasised the extent to which the Labour Party was a competitor, rather than a collaborator, with the Liberals and to insist that Labour was making genuine inroads into Liberal support. This argument rests upon analyses of Labour progress in local elections during the period 1911–14 and on studies that show that rivalry between the Liberals and Labour at local level was often intense.

The less ideologically committed historians have also contributed to the debate about the long-term survival of the Liberal Party by questioning the strength of enthusiasm for the principles of New Liberalism among traditional Liberal supporters and party activists.

Supporters of the future viability of the Liberal Party have tried, in their turn, to counter the attacks on the Wilson thesis by arguing that, but for the outbreak of war in 1914, the Liberals would have sustained or even increased their electoral appeal. Certainly there is nothing in the attitudes of the Liberal Party itself to suggest that it was lacking in confidence or living in fear of the Labour Party. After all, in 1913, the Liberal Government passed a Trade Union Act permitting trade unions to use funds for political purposes, a reversal of the Osborne Judgement of 1909 (see page 94), which had done so much to damage Labour Party funds. This was hardly the action of a government fearful of a dangerous rival.

Land reform

There is no doubt that the Liberal Government intended to embark upon a major political offensive in the period before the First World War. It was Lloyd George who supplied the strategy. In 1912 he began to revive the idea of land reform. The intention was to offer a comprehensive package of reforms, including a guaranteed minimum wage for agricultural workers with rent tribunals to ensure fair rents and, possibly, even arrange for deductions to be made directly from rental income to fund the minimum wage.

Lloyd George also intended to include urban land in the reforms, though he had no specific ideas for this more complex area. Initially, he merely indicated that he hoped that rural land reform would help to halt the flow of migrants from the land to the towns and thus help to raise urban wages. Lloyd George intended the land campaign to be the centrepiece of the Liberal revival which would carry them through the next general election, due by the end of 1915 at the latest. He set up a Land Enquiry Committee to provide detailed information and proposals. The committee, however, was not an independent group. It was a political body appointed and directed by Lloyd George and financed privately by some of his wealthy political associates.

The land campaign was specifically intended to damage the Unionists electorally. It aimed to consolidate Liberal support in the rural constituencies as well as play on the sympathies of the urban working class. It was also intended to increase divisions among the Unionists, who found it difficult to respond with land reforms of their own, without risking upsetting at least some of their supporters.

However, the need for some kind of initiative of this kind was urgent. By 1912 it was apparent that land taxation as envisaged in the 1909 Budget was never going to raise the amount of revenue needed to fund even the existing provision of social welfare, let alone any extension of it. The National Insurance scheme was far from popular with many sections of the working classes, especially the lower paid, such as agricultural labourers, who saw the contributions as a burden. Liberalism desperately needed a new electoral appeal and, by 1914, the evidence of by-elections seemed to suggest that the land campaign was having the desired effect. Moreover, the Unionists were openly divided between those supporting the Unionist Social Reform Committee, who wished to respond to Lloyd George's campaign with their own radical proposals, and members of the reactionary 'Land Union' who were still hoping to commit the Party to the repeal of the 1909 land taxes.

Irreversibly in decline?

Ultimately, the question of the strength of the Liberal Party, in 1914, must remain a matter of historical controversy. Because the First World War came when it did, the impact of the land campaign might have had on the next general election cannot be known. Similarly, it cannot be certain that the progress made by the Labour Party before 1914, at local level, provides a genuine guide to its likely fortunes in a general election. Success in local elections is not a sure indicator that similar success would be sustained in a general election. After all, the Labour Party lost a series of parliamentary by-elections between 1910 and 1914 which reduced their seats to 36 by the eve of the First World War.

On balance there would appear to be no conclusive evidence to suggest that the Liberals were already in irreversible decline in 1914. Even leading members of the Labour Party, such as Ramsay MacDonald, did not rule out an ultimate alliance with the Liberals at that stage. Similarly, the land campaign clearly shows that the Liberals were capable of developing a significant new initiative in matters of social and economic policy.

3 | British Foreign Policy and the Outbreak of War in 1914

Key question
What were the main issues that shaped British foreign policy before 1914?

The government's decision in August 1914 to enter the war against Germany on the side of France and Russia was the logical consequence of the application of long-standing principles on which foreign policy had been based for centuries. These principles can be identified as relating to the following concerns:

- strategic and security issues
- trade and commercial issues
- the balance of power and the maintenance of peace.

Strategy and security issues

In strategic and security terms, British interests required that the Royal Navy be in control of the approaches to Britain across the Atlantic and in the North Sea. Additionally the Navy was required to defend the trade routes of the Empire. This meant in particular the maintenance of control of the Mediterranean, which was essential for the protection of the Suez Canal. The Canal in turn was vital to communications with India. From at least the 1870s, India had been seen as central to the maintenance of the Empire as a whole and thus played a key role in shaping British foreign policy.

British determination to remain in control of Ireland was shaped by the fear that it could be used as a base for attacks on the British mainland if it fell under the domination of a continental power. Equally the 'Low Countries' – Belgium and Holland – were possible starting points for an invasion across the English Channel. Britain could not aim to occupy these countries but it could and did aim to ensure their independence and neutrality as the best guarantee of British strategic interests.

Trade and commercial issues

As a trading nation, Britain needed to export her produce and import raw materials for her industries. The cotton industry in particular was totally dependent on imported raw cotton and exported over three-quarters of its output. Here again the Low Countries were important. The port of Antwerp was a major trade route into Europe and its neutral status guaranteed access to markets. British trade was global and British naval supremacy was an economic issue as well as a protection against invasion.

The balance of power

The balance of power in Europe meant, from the British point of view, that no one continental power should dominate over the others. Since the Franco-Prussian War of 1871, Germany had been acknowledged as the most powerful nation in Europe and by 1900 there was already some Anglo-German tension mounting. However, during the course of the nineteenth century Britain had increasingly seen the maintenance of peace in Europe as a key objective. War, once seen as a means of gaining resources and markets, was now more generally seen as a destructive force leading to the loss of trade and the distortion of markets.

The abandonment of 'splendid isolation'

Key question
Why did Britain retreat from 'splendid isolation'?

During the period 1895–1914 the pursuit of these objectives led Britain to adopt new methods that have sometimes been described as bringing about a 'diplomatic revolution'. Until 1902 Britain maintained a policy of avoiding direct commitments to other powers in the form of specific alliances. This policy became known as 'splendid isolation' as it was based on the assumption that Britain's power was such that alliances were unnecessary and likely to lead to conflicts in which Britain had no stake.

From the late 1890s, however, a change of policy took shape. There was worldwide opposition to Britain over the Boer War and increased tension with both France and Germany in addition there was a long-standing concerns about Russian designs on India. Salisbury's government concluded that something needed to be done to reduce the potential for conflict and the risk of a major coalition of powers forming an anti-British front.

- In 1902 Britain concluded a formal alliance with Japan that helped reduce a worrying position of naval shortfall in the Far East. Japan had a strong navy.
- In 1904 an 'Entente Cordiale' or friendly understanding was reached with France. Under its terms, the two countries agreed to respect each other's interests in colonial affairs and end their rivalry overseas. It was not a formal alliance but it heralded the start of increasing co-operation between France and Britain made all the more concrete by the concerns both countries had about the increasingly erratic and aggressive behaviour emanating from Germany.
- The agreement with France was extended in 1907 to include France's ally Russia, so helping to reduce decades of hostility. Britain wanted to extend this system of agreements to include one with Germany but this failed to materialise. In 1899 and again in 1901, attempts had been made to find a basis for a general agreement with Germany and possibly even an alliance. Germany, however, wanted Britain to join the German alliance system with Austria and Italy and this Britain would not do because of the risk of being drawn into conflicts with the French and Russians.

Relations with Germany became a continuing problem. There was a clash in 1895 over the 'Jameson Raid' in southern Africa (see page 17). From the late 1890s German naval policy of expanding the German fleet caused further concern. Britain needed naval supremacy to maintain its position as a great power. Britain saw Germany as a great power in Europe with a large and modern army at its disposal. This alone might be a cause of concern. If Germany intended to challenge Britain at sea then an eventual conflict was inevitable. Diplomatic incidents in Morocco in 1905 and again in 1911 brought France and Germany into dispute and Britain was forced to take the French side. Attempts to find a basis for a naval agreement with Germany came to nothing.

The outbreak of war

Despite the concerns about Anglo-German relations, specific rivalries or tensions between Britain and Germany played almost no part in the British decision to declare war on Germany on 4 August 1914. The assassination of the Austrian Archduke Franz Ferdinand by a Bosnian Serb at Sarajevo on 28 June 1914 scarcely seemed to touch British interests at all. As late as 23 July, Lloyd George was telling the House of Commons that Anglo-German relations were better than they had been for many years.

Key question
Why did Britain go to war with Germany in August 1914?

Archduke Franz
Ferdinand and
Sophie, Duchess of
Hohenberg, riding in a
car in Sarajevo before
the assassination
which led to the First
World War because of
the alliance system.

What decided the issue was the German declaration of war
against France.

Britain was already involved in an informal naval alliance with
France, under which France would defend the Mediterranean,
and Britain the Channel and the North Sea in the event of war.
The fact that even the Cabinet knew little about the extent of
Anglo-French preparations served to create confusion and
hesitation at Cabinet level when matters drew to a head, but even
this could not ultimately affect the outcome. The fact that the fate
of Belgium lay bound up with German military plans helped to
focus the minds of the doubters, like Lloyd George, who found it
hard to countenance the horror of the impending conflict.

The Belgium question

Key question
Why was Belgium
important to Britain?

The issue of Belgium was significant because Belgian
independence was a long-standing British commitment that even
Gladstone had been willing to contemplate fighting to defend.
That Belgium was a small power facing a mighty adversary was
convenient for impressing public opinion and for staking a claim
to the moral high ground; it was not in itself decisive. Britain
could turn a blind eye to the plight of small powers faced by
aggression when it was expedient to do so.

The Germans had long planned to attack France through Belgium if war came and the reaction of the British hardly weighed with them at all in this respect. Although the Germans hoped that by some means the British might be kept out of the war they never counted on this in their planning. On the contrary, they had always assumed that they must prepare for the contingency that Britain would assist France. Since they also assumed the war would be short they attached little importance to the British threat – the British Army being, in the words of the Kaiser, 'contemptible' in terms of its size.

Nothing that Sir Edward Grey could have done in his negotiations with the Germans could have averted the eventual outcome. He has been criticised for not making the British position clear enough to the Germans. On the contrary, he made the position entirely clear: Germany was not to count on British neutrality; France and Russia were not to count on British support. This sounds paradoxical but, in diplomatic terms, it was not. A Russo-German war, not involving Britain, was theoretically possible but a Franco-German war that did not involve Britain, was not.

In practice the Germans were not concerned to avoid a war with France, so the situation remained hypothetical. For Britain the issue was clear. To stand aside was to risk allowing the complete domination of the continent of Europe by Germany. This was inconceivable on strategic and economic grounds, to say nothing of the question of British prestige. Neutrality in 1914 would have destroyed the balance of power once and for all and, with it, the independence of Great Britain.

Grey put the issue squarely to the House of Commons on 3 August 1914 before the actual declaration of war by Germany against France. Russia and Germany had been at war since 1 August and Germany had invaded Luxembourg on 2 August, at the same time demanding freedom of passage through Belgium in return for a guarantee of Belgian territorial integrity:

> I ask the House from the point of view of British interests, to consider what may be at stake. If France is beaten in a struggle of life and death, beaten to her knees, loses her position as a great Power, becomes subordinate to the will and power of one greater than herself ... If, in a crisis like this, we run away from those obligations of honour and interest as regards the Belgian Treaty, I doubt whether, whatever material force we might have at the end, it would be of very much value in face of the respect we should have lost.

4 | The Political Impact of the War

The question of Britain's entry into the war in August 1914 was divisive for the two main British parties, the Liberals and the Unionists. It was most divisive of all for the Labour Party.

Key question
Why did the First World War have such a crucial effect on the Liberal and Labour Parties?

The Liberal Party

The Liberal Party contained significant numbers of people with pacifist instincts who opposed war on moral principle. These people had to decide whether to sacrifice their views for the national interest or stick to their principles. Two Cabinet ministers did resign on these grounds. There were also some Liberals who had long admired Germany as a modern state with an advanced system of social welfare. For them the declaration of war was a particular blow. Most Liberals, however, were suspicious of German militarism and disliked the German constitution, which gave direct power to the Kaiser and his Chancellor. Most Liberals were able to support the war in principle. However, the methods of fighting it, **Total War** as it became known, with conscription and extensive state intervention in economic affairs, became very difficult for Liberals to accept.

The Conservative Party

The Conservative Party was the most united in its support for the war, but it still contained a significant minority, including some at a high level, who felt that war against Germany was a mistake. These Conservatives saw Germany, with its strongly authoritarian system of government in which the Kaiser held real power, as a bastion against revolution. In addition, they were concerned over the disruptive impact the war would have on economic and financial affairs, given that Germany was Britain's biggest trading partner.

The Labour Party

The Labour Party was the most deeply divided of all (see pages 96–8). There were those in the Party, pacifists and others, who regarded the war as essentially a capitalist conflict in which the working classes would be the victims. This view stemmed from the Marxist idea that war and imperialism were simply devices of the ruling classes to prop up declining capitalism. Despite the influence of pacifism and Marxism, however, there was also a strong patriotic response, particularly prevalent among some of the trade union leaders, which argued that ideology must take second place to national danger.

Initial war policy

Initially the Liberal Government aimed to continue in office to conduct the war along traditional lines, which meant raising volunteer armies and relying on private companies to purchase the war supplies needed for the armed forces.

The Conservatives agreed to support the government as a 'loyal opposition' for the duration of the conflict. Direct opposition came only from a minority of the more outspoken Irish Nationalist MPs and a small group of dissident Labour MPs, and even this opposition was fairly low-key. Since the press also decided to suspend political hostilities, the political status quo seemed set to be maintained.

Key term

Total War
Where all the resources of a country – human, industrial and commercial – are mobilised to serve the war effort.

However, it quickly became apparent that the government could not meet the demands of the war simply by relying on the existing industrial structure. By early 1915 there was an acute shortage of munitions of all kinds and especially artillery shells. The 'shell scandal' led to the press threatening to withdraw its support and publicly expose the shortages. The Conservatives said that if this happened they would have no alternative but also to condemn the government. The result was that, in May 1915, Asquith and the senior Liberals agreed to form a coalition government in which the leading Conservatives took Cabinet posts along with one member of the Labour Party.

Liberal decline

In December 1916, the coalition foundered. Asquith had for months been prey to depression and excessive drinking. Shattered by the death of his son on the western front, he became a pathetic shadow of the once brilliant politician he had been. His inability to provide adequate leadership led to a move within the coalition, not to oust him from the premiership as such, but to hand over the day-to-day running of the war to a new small committee headed by Lloyd George.

Lloyd George had been given the job of **Minister of Munitions** in the 1915 coalition and had made such a success of it that he was now seen on all sides as the most dynamic and effective war politician the nation possessed. Asquith refused to accept the figurehead role allotted to him in this proposal and this forced a crisis in which Lloyd George and several other Cabinet ministers threatened to resign. In the end, in 1916, Asquith himself resigned and Lloyd George became Prime Minister.

Asquith went into opposition supported by roughly two-thirds of the Liberal Party. It was a conflict that was to destroy the Liberal Party's position in the British political system and allow the Labour Party to emerge as the natural party of opposition to the Conservatives.

5 | Women and the War

One political issue that was effectively resolved by the war was the question of the female suffrage. In July 1915 the WSPU organised a great rally to demonstrate women's support for the war effort. Following the rally, Mrs Pankhurst met Lloyd George, who was by then Minister of Munitions to demand a fuller role for women in the war. As a result the following agreements were reached:

- The WSPU would suspend their demand for female suffrage for the time being.
- Women would be allowed into virtually all forms of employment, including munitions production.
- Fair minimum wage rates would be set.
- On certain types of work, where pay was determined by output, women would receive equal pay with men.

Key dates

Lloyd George forms a new coalition government: 1916

The Liberal Party splits and Asquith goes into opposition: 1916

Key term

Minister of Munitions
A completely new government department set up specifically to oversee munitions manufacture. Women were heavily recruited to work in the newly expanded factories.

Key question
How did the outbreak of war affect the position of women?

A female munitions
worker in 1917.

The vital role played by women in the war effort in the years that
followed transformed many people's perceptions of women and
their fitness for the parliamentary vote. Women engaged in many
new forms of employment that had hitherto been considered only
suitable for men. In the munitions industry, the dangers of the
work resulted in many casualties. In one incident in a munitions
factory in 1916, over 50 people were killed, most of whom were
women. In such circumstances serious resistance to the idea of the
female suffrage simply crumbled away. For example, Asquith, one
of the bitterest opponents of the idea before the war, announced
his conversion to the idea of women's political rights in 1917.

The importance of the war
Although some historians have questioned the importance of the
war in bringing forward the parliamentary vote for women, the
evidence to support the case remains compelling. It is true that
some moves for conciliatory discussions between the government
and supporters of the women's suffrage were in prospect just
before the war, but there no hard evidence that the Liberals were
prepared to adopt female suffrage as official policy. The war was
critical in overcoming the objections of those who felt that
allowing any significant female suffrage was giving in to violence.
In any case women's votes were not the only issue. The war also
overcame the last remaining objections to full voting rights for
men. In 1918 an Act for substantially extending the right to vote
was passed:

- All men over the age of 21 became entitled to vote.
- Men over the age of 19 who had seen active service in the war
  got the vote for the next general election.

- Women over 30 became entitled to vote. Before the war any such extensive proposal for the female suffrage would have been unthinkable.

Act to enfranchise all men over 21 and all women over 30: 1918

Key date

Although women had not achieved full political equality with men, this was not to be delayed for long. In 1928, a Conservative government headed by Stanley Baldwin introduced legislation to give women the vote at 21.

6 | The Social and Economic Impact of the War

Key question
How did the war affect other aspects of British society?

Women

As seen above, the war had a significant effect on the political perception of women. This was, in effect, a social change as well. Women worked with men on more equal terms and became more financially and personally independent than ever before. With men away at the front, wives and mothers became the decision-makers in the home – even if they had not been so previously.

Class

Class distinctions began to blur. The upper classes had to 'rough it' comparatively as they were deprived of the vast retinues of servants to which they were accustomed. Girls went into war work rather than domestic service – not only was the pay better, but it was a national duty. At the front men from different social classes shared a common experience of horror and hardship, which led to despair and anger in equal proportions. Unquestioning acceptance by the lower classes of deference to their social superiors was at an end – it might be accepted, but it would be questioned.

It would be absurd to suggest that class harmony in adversity ran deep or that deeply rooted social prejudices were overturned. It is fair to say that, after the war, many social barriers and conventions were readopted or at least reimposed. However, nothing could wholly eradicate the social effects of over four years of Total War. As the historian A.J.P. Taylor observed: 'The First World War cut deep into the consciousness of modern man'. After it, nothing could ever really be the same.

Economy

What was true in the social sense was even truer in economic terms. If social change was hesitant and variable, the economic impact was bold and thorough. It quickly became apparent in 1914 that a modern war could not be fought without government intervention.

Initially the government passed a Defence of the Realm Act that gave it control of the armaments factories, but little was done to increase output. The resulting shell shortages led to a drastic rethink, which enabled Lloyd George to build munitions production to the required level.

Government intervention, however, went much further than just munitions. To fight a Total War, the whole population and the entire economic resources of the nation had to be mobilised. Vast sums of money had to be raised and deployed. Labour had to be

Nationalisation
The taking over by the government of private companies so that they are owned by the state.

directed and controlled. Output had to be specified and delivered on time. To achieve victory the financial and economic life of the nation had to be planned. To be effective, planning had to be supported and carried through by state power.

In 1915, a new Defence of the Realm Act gave the government virtually total control of the labour force and the economic resources of the country. Also in 1915, the trade unions, in return for guarantees on wages and conditions, reached an understanding with Lloyd George called the 'Treasury Agreements' in which they agreed to a no-strike arrangement so long as the war lasted. In order to increase efficiency while the war lasted, the unions also agreed to relax the usual restrictive working practices. A vast amount of government money was pumped into every aspect of war production. From being a largely food-importing nation in 1914, Britain became 80 per cent self-sufficient in food by 1918. The mining industry was effectively **nationalised** during the war. Government controls were imposed on wages, employment conditions, profits and prices.

Such a massive transformation of the economy could not be wholly reversed at the end of the war. Even though there was initially an attempt to restore pre-war conditions, post-war governments found themselves increasingly compelled to intervene in economic matters.

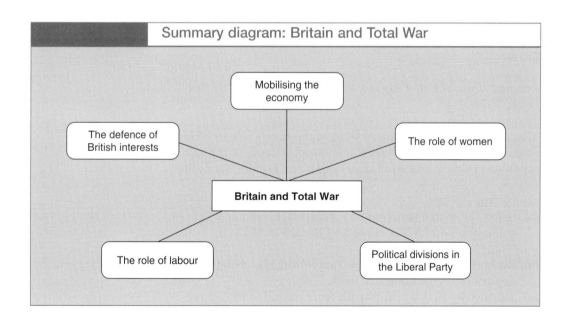

Summary diagram: Britain and Total War

- Mobilising the economy
- The defence of British interests
- The role of women
- **Britain and Total War**
- The role of labour
- Political divisions in the Liberal Party

Summary diagram: The impact of the First World War

Women

The position of women had changed forever. Although they could not, for the most part, hold on to the types of jobs they had done during the war even though they now had the vote the experience of war had destroyed the idea that men were the fountain of all wisdom.

Government

Government had interfered in the everyday lives of individuals and the affairs of private businesses to a degree that would have been unthinkable before the war.

Labour Party

The Labour Party had emerged as a participant in government and a future contender to govern Britain.

Liberal Party

The Liberal Party had suffered irreparable damage in an internal division that finished it as a party of government in its own right.

Study Guide: AS Questions

In the style of AQA

Read the following source and then answer the questions that follow.

Adapted from: War and Society in Britain 1899–1948, *by Rex Pope, 1991.*

The demands of war enhanced sharply the state's role in relation to the individual. This was seen at its most extreme in the case of munitions workers and adult males of an age suitable for military service.

(a) Using the source and your own knowledge, comment on 'military service' in the context of Britain in 1915–16.
(3 marks)
(b) Explain the ways in which the First World War changed the opportunities for women at work. (7 marks)
(c) 'During the First World War the state extended its control over the social and economic life of Britain.' Explain in what ways and why this happened. (15 marks)

Source: AQA, January 2001

Exam tips

The cross-references are intended to take you straight to the material that will help you to answer the questions.

(a) The source is really only a prompt here so using it to answer the question can be merely a matter of picking up some obvious elaboration of the quote. In this case the reference to 'males of an age suitable for military service' helps to push forward the context of conscription that lies behind the term. Your own knowledge is needed to draw out the detailed context of the controversy over conscription and the public perceptions that affected the government's decision on the issue.

(b) Focus on two aspects of this (pages 136–7):

- The disappearance of men into the armed services, which created vacancies in jobs where either men had always predominated or where women had been progressively pushed out in previous decades – shop work and agriculture, respectively, are good examples.
- The second aspect is where the war created demand that could only be met by the mobilisation of women into the workforce – munitions is the best example of this.

(c) Make sure you obtain a balance of social and economic controls. Keep referring to the needs of 'Total War' in your answer. Social controls would include such things as the dilution of beer to reduce drunkenness and the accompanying restrictions on opening hours of licensed premises (pages 138–9). Some issues like the treasury agreements between the government and the trade unions are a mixture of both economic and social control, so don't be alarmed if you have some doubts about classifying them – focus on showing what happened and what problem or objective each action was intended to address.

In the style of Edexcel

In what ways did Lloyd George influence the priorities and policies
of the Liberal governments of 1905–15?   (30 marks)

Source: Edexcel, January 2004

Exam tips

Pay attention to the need to comment on the relative importance of the
factors you identify and to establish linkage between them as far as
possible. As President of the Board of Trade Lloyd George was directly
involved in an outstanding record of legislative achievement. He
introduced measures on merchant shipping, company administration,
along with regulations on designs and patents and a major overhaul of
the Port of London Authority. As a result of his achievements he was
the logical choice to succeed Asquith as Chancellor of the Exchequer
when the latter became Prime Minister in 1908. He then took over the
Old Age Pensions proposals from Asquith and saw them through to
the Statute Book before taking on the Budget of 1909. He took a
leading role in the struggle to pass the Parliament Bill in 1910–11 and
then went on the create a major modernisation of the welfare system
with the National Insurance legislation of 1911. Thereafter until the
outbreak of war he focused mainly on maintaining the economic and
financial equilibrium of the government's policy as events centred on
the Irish Crisis. Lloyd George was only ever lukewarm on the issue of
Irish Home Rule. He approved of it in principle but he never saw it as
an issue that was fundamental to Liberalism. In the period 1911–14 he
worked on proposals for agricultural and industrial regeneration but
these failed to materialise due to the outbreak of war. Lloyd George's
pre-war priorities were (a) to secure the acceptance of a greater degree
of government intervention in economic and social affairs, and (b) to
redistribute wealth through social and taxation policy. These were
controversial issues for the Liberal Party and Lloyd George was highly
influential in steering the Party firmly in that direction. Lloyd George
had doubts about entering the war but once convinced of the need, he
used his influence with the radical wing of the Liberal Party to promote
the government's case. Once the war began, his one priority was to
secure victory. In 1914–15 he focused on setting up the economy and
financial system of the country to meet the needs of a major war. He
arranged new regulations on borrowing and taxation and entered into
complex agreements with banks and financial institutions (such as
insurance companies) to ensure that there would be financial stability.
He also negotiated with the Trade Unions to achieve more flexible
working practices and a no-strike agreement for the duration of the
war. His personal credibility as Chancellor and his position as a
progressive radical were crucial to the success of these arrangements.
In his work as Minister of Munitions he showed awesome skills of
organisation in building up the ministry from nothing and increasing the
production of armaments from the point where they had been
inadequate for the British army to supplying allies with much of the
their needs. He also showed a ruthless determination to carry through
his policies.

In the style of WJEC

To what extent was the German invasion of Belgium the reason for Britain's declaration of war against Germany in August 1914?

Exam tips

The cross-references are intended to take you straight to the material that will help you to answer the question.

Follow the standard guidance for evaluative essays. Here the issue raised in the statement clearly formed the official reason given for the declaration of war and you need to develop a detailed explanation of why the neutrality of Belgium was an issue for Britain. However, you should be aware that behind the public emphasis on Belgium there was also concern about other factors (pages 131–2):

- The concern about the intentions of Germany and growing German dominance in Europe.
- The need to maintain the independence of France and the increasing collaboration with France that had marked the period from 1904.
- The view that a great power such as Britain could not afford to allow a war in Europe possibly to redraw the map of Europe in the future without reference to Britain's interests.

These factors need to be explained and balanced against the issue of Belgium in a clear overall judgement. Remember that marks for content and approach are awarded separately to make up the total score.

Glossary

Anglican   One who accepts the doctrine of the Anglican Church of England.

Anglican schools   Originally called 'National Schools', these schools provided elementary education and were sponsored by the Church of England.

Annexations   Territory taken by the winner from the loser.

Autocracy   A system where one person has absolute rule.

Boers   Descendants of the original Dutch-speaking farmers who had first colonised the Cape and who had migrated north to escape the rule of the British. Boer in Dutch means farmer.

Budget deficit   Occurs when more is being spent than raised in taxes – a gap that can only be filled by borrowing.

Cabinet   The highest level of government, the members of which run the most important government departments.

Capitalist system   Economic system based on private ownership of land and resources and driven by the need to make profits.

Class struggle   A continuing conflict at every stage of history between those who possessed economic and political power and those who did not, in simple terms the 'haves' and the 'have-nots'.

Coalition   A coming together of different groups or political parties. Many countries are governed by coalition governments, but this is unusual in Britain.

Conscription   Compulsory military service.

Conservatism   The political principle that the presentation of traditions and existing institutions should be assumed to be the objective of politics.

Constitutional crisis   A political crisis where the issues provoking the crisis relate to the rules under which the country is governed.

Corn Laws   Laws originally introduced in 1815 to tax cereal products coming into the country in order to protect domestic farmers from foreign competition.

Death duty   Taxes levied on the property or money left by a person when they die.

Disestablishment   The principle of separating the Church of England from its legal connection with the Constitution.

Elementary education   Compulsory basic education provided up to the age of 11 or 12 for all children.

Female suffrage   The right of women to vote in parliamentary elections.

Fenian   Late-nineteenth-century group of Irish Nationalists whose aim was Irish independence. They organised a rising in 1827 and carried out bombings in British cities. They recruited heavily in the USA from Irish immigrants.

Foreign Secretary   The Cabinet minister responsible for handling the country's relations with foreign powers and its responses to international events.

Franchise   The terms on which individuals hold the right to vote.

Free trade   An economic policy in which taxes are not applied (or only minimally applied) to imports and exports and no barriers are imposed on the import or export of goods.

Friendly societies and **Industrial insurance companies**   Types of insurance company providing policies at cheap rates to enable to the less well off to provide for funeral, sickness expenses or injuries suffered at work.

Great Reform Act   An act that set standard voting qualifications in rural and urban constituencies, increasing numbers of votes from around 450,000 to 500,000.

Great Victorian Boom   An expression customarily used to describe the expansion of production in agriculture and industry during the period 1850–70.

Home Rule   The principle that Ireland should control its own *internal* affairs within the United Kingdom.

Humanitarian   Concern for the human condition and especially for those thought to be unable to protect themselves.

Imperial federation   The principle of joining several self-governing territories within the Empire into a union of equals.

Imperial unification   Bringing the 'mother' country (Britain) into closer economic and political unity with dominions and colonies.

Imperialist   The principle of territorial expansion by a country in order to strengthen its position.

Indemnities   Compensation paid by the losers to the winners to cover, partly or in full, their war costs. The term 'reparations' is often used to describe this.

Interventionist social reform   Reforms relying on direct action by Government to enforce conditions.

Invisible earnings   Earnings from insurance premiums, shipping and brokerage fees, where no actual sale of goods was involved.

Irish Nationalists   Those Irish politicians who demanded greater (or even full) independence for Ireland from Great Britain.

Juvenile court   Law courts dealing only with offences committed by children.

Labour exchanges   Government offices where the unemployed could be helped to find work.

Labour historians   Historians who generally see the rise of the Labour Party as an inevitable (and welcome) process.

Labour movement   Principle of organising the working classes so that they can achieve better conditions.

Landlordism   System of land use where real power resides with those who own the land at the expense of those who actually work on it.

Left-wing historians   Historians tending to reach their conditions based on their political preference for Marxist-Socialist policies.

Liberalism   The political idea that personal freedom was the best way to promote the welfare of both individuals and the nation. Gladstone, the Liberal Prime Minister, particularly emphasised that this should also mean minimal interference by the state and minimal taxation. His view has become known as 'Gladstonian Liberalism'. More radical Liberals disagreed and wanted state intervention to help the disadvantaged.

Marginal seat   Constituency where the MP has only a small majority and there is a real possibility of its being won by another MP from a different party.

Marxist   Followers of the ideas of Karl Marx, who argued that revolution was required in order to overthrow capitalism and create a classless socialist society.

Marxist historians   Historians who accept Marx's view that political and social evolution towards a Communist society is inevitable.

Militarism   Principle that military power is a desirable end in itself and that its use to achieve objectives is desirable.

Minister of Munitions   A completely new government department set up specifically to oversee munitions manufacture. Women were heavily recruited to work in the newly expanded factories.

Municipal boroughs   Boroughs with the right to elect their own town councils under an Act of 1835.

Nationalisation   The taking over by the government of private companies so that they are owned by the state.

Nonconformist   Member of any Protestant Christian Church (i.e. not a Roman Catholic) that did not 'conform' to the teachings of the Anglican Church of England. Presbyterians, Methodists and Baptists are examples.

Old Whig   Those Liberals who had originally been part of the Whig Party, itself of aristocratic background.

Partition   The separation of a single area into two or more distinct areas under separate authority.

Plural voting   An individual's right to vote in more than one constituency, e.g. if the place of residence and ownership of business premises were in two different areas.

Poverty line   The level of income needed to support the minimum requirements of life in terms of food, accommodation, etc. Obviously this would vary according to family size.

Private Member's Bill   All MPs have a right to introduce bills on their own initiative, which, if passed, become law. In the nineteenth century it was very common for even major pieces of legislation to be sponsored in this way by individual MPs rather than the government and sometimes even in defiance of the government. This virtually died out during the twentieth century and the very few Private Member's Bills that are allowed in any session can only succeed with the government's agreement.

Progressive   Prepared to introduce reform.

Protective tariffs   Taxes on imports to make them more expensive and thus 'protect' domestic produce.

Public health   A general term relating to issues such as disease, sanitation, living and working conditions and pollution.

Radical liberalism   Liberals who wanted significant changes to the existing social system in order to directly benefit the working classes.

Radicalism   Radicalism was a term applied generally to those who believed that the political, social and economic systems of the country needed reform of a very significant degree – changing very basic things such as how poverty was relieved or who should have the right to vote.

Real wages   Define the value of goods or services that wages can actually buy. For example, if wages remain the same while food prices increase, their 'real' value has gone down. On the other hand if food prices fall the 'real' value of wages has risen.

Remand home   Detention centres where children convicted of offences could be sent to learn and develop rather than being sent to prison.

Republican   One who rejects the principle of monarchy in favour of a head of state elected by or appointed from the people of the country.

Resolutions   Statements that are voted upon in principle but which, if passed, have no force in law.

Royal Commission   Set up to investigate a particular issue and usually to suggest a course of action. Generally composed of a mixture of politicians, interested parties and experts in whatever field under enquiry.

Sanatorium   A kind of hospital especially for recovery from long-term debilitating conditions. Emphasis was placed on rest, cleanliness and good ventilation.

'Scorched earth' policy   A military tactic in which buildings, crops, livestock, factories, etc., are destroyed in order to deprive the opposition of resources.

Secondary education   Further non-compulsory education, usually only undertaken by middle class or better-off working-class children, which ended at any age up to 18.

Selective breeding programmes   The principle of ensuring that only those who are free from disease and hereditary defects are allowed to reproduce.

Separatism   Principle of separating Ireland from Great Britain.

Sinking fund   A government fund into which money is put for paying off government debts as they become due for repayment.

Social insurance   The provision of support to those unable to look after themselves.

Social reform   The introduction of new laws to improve social conditions.

Socialism   A social and economic system in which private property in all forms is abolished and the means of production and distribution of wealth are owned by the community as a whole.

Socialist   The political principle that requires the abolition of private property in favour of public ownership.

Socialist Workers' Republic   Political system where government is based on the principle of a socialist state controlled by the working classes.

Stamp duty   A tax paid to the government for legalising official or legal documents, e.g. on the sale of property.

State pension   Money paid to people over a certain age out of state funds.

Total War   Where all the resources of a country – human, industrial and commercial – are mobilised to serve the war effort.

Trade gap   Where the value of items imported into the country exceed the value of exports.

Unionism   Unionists were those who argued that the Union between Great Britain and Ireland must be kept at all costs and that any measure of Home Rule for Ireland was bound to lead to separation in the long run.

Veto   The right to reject a bill completely.

West Britonism   The idea that Ireland had no real separate identity but was merely a geographical area of Britain.

Whips   MPs who within their own political party, ensure that the other MPs vote according to the wishes of the party leadership. If the party is in government, the whips are paid members of the government.

Index